QUINTESSENTIALLY
RESERVE 2013

Aditya Resort ◆ Al Maha Desert Resort and Spa ◆ Almyra ◆ Aman Sveti Stefan
Amankila ◆ Amankora ◆ Amanpuri ◆ Amanyara ◆ Ananda in the Himalayas
Anassa ◆ Ararat Park Hyatt Moscow ◆ Armani Hotel Dubai ◆ Asimina Suites
Awasi ◆ Banyan Tree Madivaru ◆ Baros Maldives Resort & Spa ◆ Blanket Bay
Blantyre ◆ Brown's Hotel ◆ Caesar Augustus ◆ Canouan Island ◆ Cap Juluca
Carlton Hotel St Moritz ◆ Castello di Casole ◆ Castiglion del Bosco ◆ Chateau de Bagnols
China World Summit Wing ◆ Clayoquot Wilderness Resort ◆ Coco Palm Bodu Hithi
Colony Palms Hotel ◆ Conrad Pezula ◆ Cuixmala ◆ Danai Beach Resort & Villas
Diamonds Star of the East ◆ DPNY Beach Hotel ◆ Eagles Nest ◆ Eolo
Exploreans Mara Rianta ◆ Faena Hotel ◆ Fairmont Pacific Rim ◆ Finca Cortesin Hotel & Golf
Frégate Island Private ◆ Fuchun Resort ◆ Fullerton Bay Hotel ◆ Fusion Maia Da Nang
Grace Santorini ◆ Grand Hotel Bellevue ◆ Grand Hotel du Cap Ferrat
Grand Hotel Tremezzo Palace ◆ Gstaad Palace ◆ Hotel Arlberg ◆ Hotel d'Angleterre
Hotel Danieli ◆ Hotel d'Inghilterra ◆ Hotel Esencia ◆ Hotel Gritti Palace
Hotel Hacienda Ibiza ◆ Hotel Le Bristol Paris ◆ Icehotel ◆ Il Pellicano ◆ Indigo Pearl
Jumeirah Dhevanafushi ◆ Jumeirah Vittaveli ◆ Kenoa Resort ◆ Kensington Place
La Posta Vecchia ◆ Le Burgundy ◆ Le Manoir Aux Quat'Saisons ◆ Le Meurice
Les Suites De La Potiniere ◆ Les Trois Rois ◆ Lydmar Hotel
Mandarin Oriental New York ◆ Mandarin Oriental Paris ◆ Maradiva
Masseria San Domenico ◆ Museum Hotel Cappadocia ◆ Mzima ◆ Necker Island
Palace Hotel Tokyo ◆ Paresa ◆ Park Hyatt Jeddah ◆ Park Hyatt Maldives
Park Hyatt Zurich ◆ Parrot Cay ◆ Pine Cliffs Terraces & Villas ◆ Pousada Estrela D'Água
Princess D'an Nam Resort and Spa ◆ Qualia ◆ Royal Riviera ◆ San Domenico House
Sha Wellness Clinic ◆ Shangri-La Hotel Paris ◆ Shangri-La Singapore ◆ Shangri-La Villingili
Shangri-La's Boracay Resort & Spa ◆ Silavadee Pool Spa & Resort ◆ Singita Grumeti Reserves
Singita Sabi Sand ◆ Sparkling Hill ◆ St Regis Bali ◆ St Regis Bangkok ◆ St Regis Beijing
St Regis New York ◆ St. Regis Mauritius ◆ St. Regis Saadiyat ◆ The Augustine ◆ The Betsy
The Chatwal ◆ The Connaught ◆ The Fortress ◆ The Fullerton Hotel ◆ The Halkin
The Island Shangri-La ◆ The Kensington Hotel ◆ The Milestone Hotel ◆ The Mulia Nusa Dua, Bali
The Naka Island ◆ The Peninsula Hong Kong ◆ The Plaza ◆ The Racha ◆ The Setai Miami Beach
The Sofa Hotel ◆ Treehotel ◆ Trianon Palace Versailles ◆ Tribe Hotel ◆ Txai Resort
Uma by Como ◆ W Retreat & Spa Bali ◆ W Singapore Sentosa Cove ◆ W South Beach

QUINTESSENTIALLY
RESERVE 2013

*A hand-picked collection of the world's
most luxurious hotels and retreats*

QUINTESSENTIALLY
PUBLISHING

QUINTESSENTIALLY TRAVEL GROUP

Aviation | Escape | Travel | Villas

YOUR TAILOR-MADE PASSPORT TO THE WORLD

www.quintessentiallytravel.com
reserve@quintessentiallytravel.com

LONDON
+44 (0) 845 269 1152

NEW YORK
+1 212 206 6633

HONG KONG
+852 2540 8595

DUBAI
+971 4 437 6802

WELCOME

It is a great pleasure to welcome you to Quintessentially Reserve 2013, the seventh edition of our guide to the world's most exclusive, luxurious hotels and unique holiday retreats. From the most glamorous hotels in the metropolis of New York City to your very own Private Island in the Caribbean surrounded by pristine nature; there is something to suit everyone's taste. You'll gasp at the luxury safari lodges, amble through great chateaux and manors, pad contentedly along powdery white sand beaches, and swim in crystal-clear waters. We have taken great care in selecting each property to give any discerning traveller all of the inspiration they need for their next adventures around the globe. Quintessentially Reserve can be found on the shelves of some of the most prestigious stores around the world, and is known as the very best in the luxury travel book genre. It will also be available online and as an e-book. As you leaf through these pages, indulging in your wildest dreams, we will take you on an exciting journey around the world, as seen through the eyes of Quintessentially Reserve.

Project Manager - *Hallie Bird*

CONTENTS

THE AMERICAS
EUROPE
AFRICA
MIDDLE EAST
INDIAN OCEAN
ASIA
PACIFIC

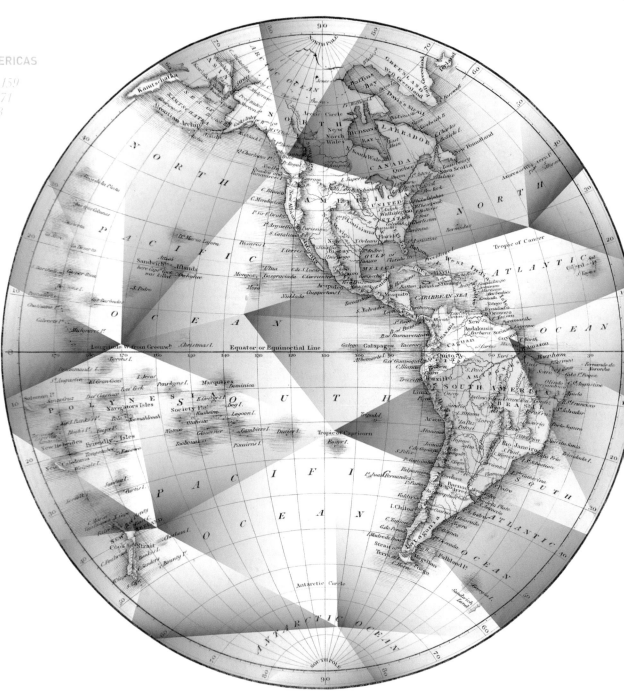

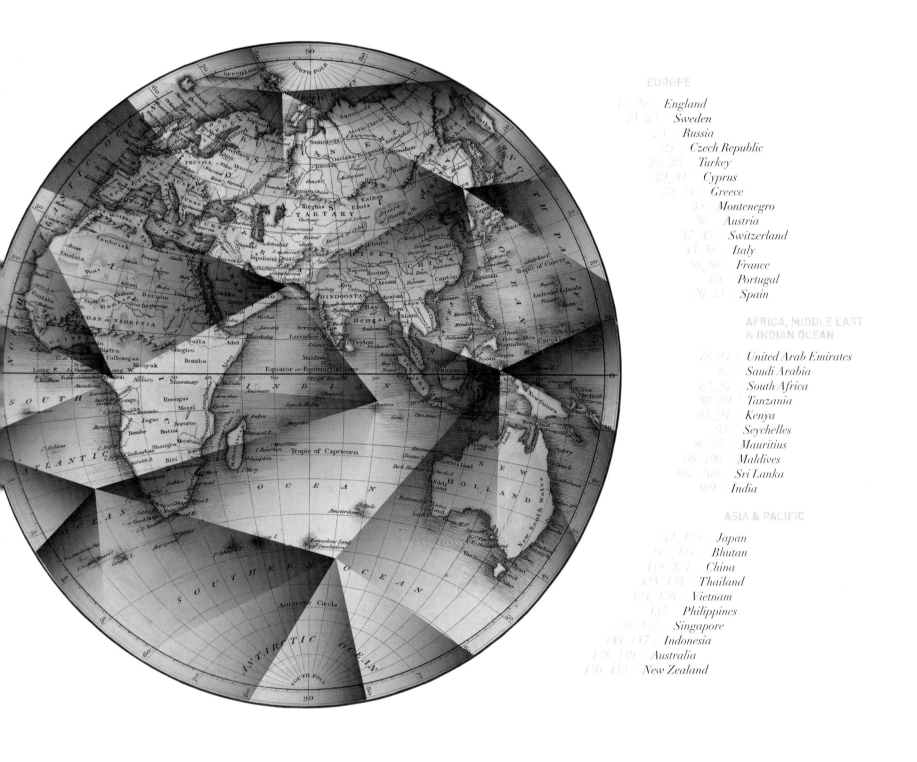

CONTENTS EUROPE

LE MANOIR **AUX QUAT'SAISONS**

Oxfordshire / *England*

Le Manoir aux Quat'Saisons is one of those rare addresses you can return to and have a totally fresh experience. The hotel's restaurant was awarded two Michelin stars in 1985 and has held them ever since- a remarkable feat in such a competitive and ever-changing business. All 32 rooms and suites are uniquely different, from Lemongrass to the seductive red-bedecked Opium, to the split-level Dovecote with its romantic, 15th-century architecture. You also get a completely different gourmet extravaganza every time; that's because Le Manoir is the country seat of Super-chef Raymond Blanc. The man isn't one of those who simply adds his name to a five-star hotel; he also has a cooking school here, so when you see him walking around the hotel, be sure to strike up a conversation. The menu showcases the power of understatement (the kitchens are largely supplied by Le Manoir's organic gardens, which form part of the property's 27 acres).

Surrounded by lawns, flower borders and orchards, the setting is idyllic and celebrates a typically English style. Oozing quintessential rural charm from its honey-coloured gables, the hotel is seven miles from Oxford and a 90-minute drive from Central London.

La Belle Époque is Le Manoir's private dining room. It opens up onto an enchanting walled garden within the oldest part of the house and is perfect for a private celebration or a business event.

BROWN'S **HOTEL**

London | England

Brown's Hotel is one of the most stylish addresses in London. Nestled in the heart of Mayfair, it has - since its opening as London's first ever hotel in 1837- been a fashionable hotspot for opinion leaders and celebrities -from Winston Churchill and Rudyard Kipling to David Cameron and Stella McCartney. Everyone is a VIP here though. The hotel's concierge team will make you feel utterly at home - being able to choose your perfect pillow is a lovely touch. After a trip round the city's boutiques– Bond Street and Regent Street are just minutes away –the hotel's award-winning Afternoon Tea is just the ticket with a selection of teas, sumptuous sandwiches and freshly-baked cakes. There's a complimentary sample of tea to take away that completes this quintessentially English experience.

Renowned for its sense of innovation and taste, the hotel celebrates world-class cuisine against a backdrop of jaw dropping British art. HIX Mayfair showcases work from Tracey Emin and Michael Landy as a stunning setting for the dining experience, while The Donovan Bar pays homage to iconic photographer Terence Donovan, even dedicating a 'naughty corner' to a series of his more risqué prints!

Despite its sleek and sophisticated lines this hotel is family friendly with activities and facilities to allow everyone to enjoy the experience - interconnecting rooms and kids' programmes for example.

The hotel's motto: "Once a guest of Brown's, always a guest of Brown's" echoes in your mind long after checking out and make no mistake- it's the only place to be and be seen.

THE **CONNAUGHT**

London | England

Coveted heritage, superior cuisine, a priceless location – the Connaught has been standing proud at the heart of Mayfair for over a century. Sat on the corner of Mount Street and Carlos Place, this handsome hotel is the epitome of British luxury. Thanks to a recent multi-million pound renovation, original features combine with contemporary design to create unrivalled splendour.

Two Michelin-starred Hélène Darroze's eponymous restaurant channels authentic regional and seasonal flavours from her native home of south-west France. Darroze's signature nine-course menu is an exquisite example of French haute cuisine. After dinner, the ultra-stylish Connaught Bar beckons. Designed by David Collins, the menu is a fusion of tradition and innovation using exclusive vintages and premier crus to create award-winning cocktails. For something

more intimate, try settling down in one of the Coburg Bar's sumptuous velvet armchairs for a night cap.

However, the Connaught's real treasures are hidden underground. Beneath the kitchen lies the Connaught's renowned limestone-clad cellar, housing some 6000 vintage wines. Here, the exclusive Sommelier's Table provides private dining perfect for oenophiles who want to experience the hotel's unique cellar. Aman Spa, a revitalising haven dedicated to holistic well-being, is also subterranean. Drawing inspiration from ancient cultures and customs, its candle-lit signature treatments are personalised, making it the most luxurious retreat in Mayfair.

Don't miss Afternoon Tea in Espelette's stunning curved conservatory. It's perfectly positioned for

admiring "Silence", Carlos Place's mesmerizing new water feature designed by Tadao Ando.

THE MILESTONE **HOTEL**

London / *England*

Just a few steps away from Princess Diana and Queen Victoria's old stomping grounds, stands an iconic hotel that tips its hat to the history surrounding it. The Milestone Hotel offers quite a different take on London that draws on its illustrious surroundings. South Kensington is the essence of elegance which must be why the royal family moved into the neighbourhood in the 17th century.

The first treat as you arrive at The Milestone is a complimentary glass of champagne from your personal butler (what a way to be greeted!),

after which you're taken on a personal tour of the hotel. To get in the mood of the place, why not take tea in the conservatory or have a drink in the juxtaposing Stables Bar and sink into the leather armchairs? One of the best places to get a sense of this extraordinary hotel's character is in The Park Lounge. Its impressive walls are lined with leather bound books and oversized portraits that command a peaceful hush.

No two rooms have the same décor though they all boast warmth of colour and texture. We particularly

love the little touches, like the homemade cookies, bonbons and canapés that appear in your room twice a day. Another bonus? The Milestone offers a special service for families and pets (pooch can be pampered too), so be sure to take advantage of a fully accredited nanny for the children and behind-the-scenes tours to keep them happy.

Cheneston's Restaurant serves some of Britain's best, modern cuisine. The Irish and Scottish smoked salmon and the savoury English asparagus are just some of the highlights on the menu. For more private meals, the adjoining and elaborately decorated oratory will hold up to eight guests and the sommelier will recommend the perfect wines to complement your meal. Many of the rooms have a view of Kensington Gardens – great for long walks and contemplation away from city life. Enjoy a picnic outside the palace before walking to some of Britain's most loved museums as well as word-class boutiques including Harrods. If you don't feel up to walking, use the Milestone's chauffeur-driven Bentley and make the most of the hotel's outstanding hospitality.

Your stay is guaranteed to leave you feeling like royalty.

SAN DOMENICO **HOUSE**

London | England

Checking in at San Domenico House in the heart of Chelsea is much like coming home. With an inviting combination of contemporary flair and lavish home from home comfort comes guaranteed privacy – there are just 16 rooms and suites. You'll always be greeted by name and with a warm smile (some may argue this is better than home!) and staff will attend to your every need 24/7.

The décor is lavish and chosen with exquisite taste- antique furniture, classic pieces of art on every wall and staircases with more than a touch of originality. The bespoke room service, attentive breakfast dining, and luxurious bathrooms will make you wish you were staying longer. Be sure to spend some time on the roof terrace with a drink - a chance to take in the fabulous London skyline. With the city's finest shopping nearby and the green open spaces of Hyde Park to explore San Domenico House is a genuine little treasure.

THE KENSINGTON **HOTEL**

London | England

A visit to the Kensington guarantees you a prime central London location and a piece of the Regency-style townhouse experience. The bedrooms and suites are like individual boutiques within themselves, housing designer furniture from George Smith and Julian Chichester.

Bay-windowed drawing rooms are crowned with ornate fireplaces, and provide the ideal environment for enjoying The Kensington's renowned afternoon tea. Pay a visit to Aubrey, the luxurious club-like restaurant offering true British Cuisine created by a talented culinary team.

Particularly impressive is the cocktail bar, promising the best Martini in town courtesy of top mixologist Alessandro Pizzoli. Distressed mirrors, timber-clad walls, slate floors and a spectacular ceiling of blue

glass set the tone for the highest quality night you're likely to enjoy for quite some time.

The stylish Knightsbridge and Chelsea shopping stretches are not to be missed, particularly given their proximity to the hotel. Minutes away are Hyde Park and Kensington Gardens, world-class attractions including the V & A, the Royal Albert Hall and the Natural History and Science Museums.

THE HALKIN **BY COMO**

London / *England*

Tucked away in London's chic Belgravia is the gem that is The Halkin by COMO. A most pleasant surprise with its slick, modern décor (in contrast to its Georgian exterior) this extraordinary place is something of a close-kept secret among urban retreat lovers.

Sleek bedrooms and suites designed by Laboratorio Associati Italy reflect the mood throughout. Cosseting lighting, integrated mod-cons (flat screen plasma and touch screen consoles) and floor-to-ceiling marble bathrooms coupled with sensual silks and linens, comforting wool and calming taupes and creams make it hard to believe you're in the centre of a buzzing capital city (Mayfair's restaurants, Hyde Park, Sloane Street and Piccadilly's theatres are a stone's throw away).

Nahm's exquisite Thai cuisine from world-class chef David Thompson and The Halkin Bar's cocktails and nightcaps are tempting enough to keep you holed up here all evening. This is no mean feat given the proximity of the hotel to the best London has to offer, a stay here buys a share of Belgravia prestige and easy access to Knightsbridge shopping.

LYDMAR **HOTEL**

Stockholm / Sweden

Lydmar Hotel sits in the heart of Stockholm and boasts some unique added values that set it apart from other 5-star venues. The hotel philosophy rejects formality and conservative stiffness (no staff uniforms here) in favour of a calming simplicity. Staff are encouraged to express personality – you'll get the most interesting tips and insider knowledge on the city's hotspots from those who look after you here.

Rooms range from classic to extra-large and no two rooms have the same look– think individuality not conformity. The feel is contemporary chic and it's the little touches that make you feel at home. From exquisite Italian bed linen to local snacks, with breakfast in your room free of charge – you're ready to hit Stockholm with your batteries fully charged.

Don't leave without sampling the local cuisine in-house. The restaurant menu offers locally sourced food with servings as generous as the food is mouth-watering.

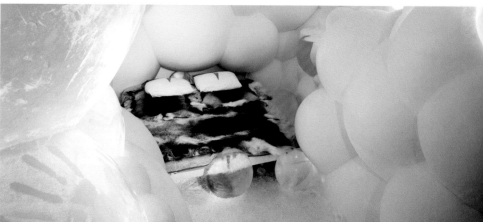

ICEHOTEL
Jukkasjärvi / *Sweden*

This winter season 2012/2013 will see the 23rd ICEHOTEL make its dramatic appearance in the small village of Jukkasjärvi in Northern Sweden. For the uninitiated, ICEHOTEL is the world's first and largest hotel, re-built every year entirely from natural snow and ice. Over more than 20 years, there have been many developments for what started as an igloo and exhibition, to what it has now become - the world's largest hotel at about 5500 square metres. This hotel is far more than a clever concept though. It's a life changing experience and every year is a new build. All of the ice art is original, handmade and created not just by professional ice craftsmen but by artists from all walks of life (sculptors, designers, photography stylists for example). Founded on natural ice harvested from the Torne River, ICEHOTEL is a leading producer of ice events around the world namely with the mother of all ICEBARs.

This is a place you absolutely must make the pilgrimage to in your lifetime. Two hundred kilometres from the Arctic Circle, you'll catch the Northern Lights you've always meant to see and where else can you dance on a floor of snow and drink champagne from an ice glass? The fact that the guests return year on year is testament to the natural spectacle that it is but also to the warm and friendly staff on hand 24 hours a day. You'll almost forget that baby, it's cold outside...

TREEHOTEL

Harads / Sweden

Remember when you were little and you begged your parents for a tree house? The contemporary Treehotel in the woods of Sweden offers both children and adults the tree house experience of their dreams. The Treehotel's guest rooms are built into the treetops of a forest, high above the ground.

This hotel allows guests to feel connected with nature with spectacular views of the surrounding forest as well as the Lule River.

Treehotel was inspired by the film "The Tree Lover" by Jonas Selberg Augustsen. It is a story of three men from the city who want to get to grips with mankind by building a tree house together. Scandinavia's leading architects ran with this concept and created 24 futuristic-looking rooms for the forest area around the remote village of Harads.

Don't worry though; this is not as rustic as your classic childhood tree house. The guest rooms are powered with electricity, supplied locally from green hydroelectric power. (There's running water too!) These guesthouses were built with the utmost concern for the environment.

The tree houses are all unique and quite eye-catching. There are five different designs including The Mirrorcube, a hideout camouflaged by mirrored walls that reflect their surroundings, and The UFO. The latter is a four-person tree house that literally looks like a spaceship landed in the trees.

To make your stay even more comfortable, there is even a tree sauna situated among the centuries-old pines. So come discover nature in an entirely new light—without a camping tent or flashlight.

ARARAT **PARK HYATT MOSCOW**

Moscow / Russia

Up on the magnificently modern Rooftop Bar - with a delicious vodka on the rocks in hand - it becomes immediately clear to any discerning traveller that the Ararat Park Hyatt Moscow is a cut above the rest. With the bustling city but a distant hum below, this establishment provides a welcome oasis of tranquillity in the midst of buzzing hub of modern innovation.

The hotel's renovation was spearheaded by renowned architect Tony Chi and the results are undeniably superb. Guests are whisked up from the lobby by the chrome-and-glass elevators (which lend a vaguely futuristic feel to the spacious reception) to rooms that ensconce every individual in luxurious cosiness. Glittering glass, panels of rich, smoked oak and plush ivory rugs blend to create an experience of warm, familiar hospitality

and comfort. The jewel-like suites, of which there are 32, are studies in consummate indulgence, and have discreet separate entrances for guests and staff. For the ultimate in luxury (and who wouldn't want that?) inquire about the Presidential Suite. Panoramic windows look out over the stunning sprawl of Moscow; the iconic Kremlin and the Red Square are just steps from the Ararat.

After a busy day exploring, refresh yourself in the indoor swimming pool (one of the hotel's best kept secrets) or pamper yourself with a spa treatment. If you don't fancy venturing back out for dinner then there's something for everyone in the hotel's three restaurants. Any stereotypical preconceptions you may have of Moscow as a cold and daunting destination will be blown away when you stay here.

THE **AUGUSTINE**

Prague / *Czech Republic*

It seems an unusual juxtaposition: an elegant boutique hotel that houses a working monastery, but the Rocco Forte Augustine Hotel Prague makes this unique union work. Where else can you experience a private monk-guided tour through a working monastery and chapel, connected to a luxury hotel? Don't pass up this exceptional opportunity! Tucked away in a peaceful area of Prague's Lesser Town, the hotel is housed in a complex of seven interconnected buildings, dated between the 13th & 16th centuries. The location immerses you in the history of this fascinating city, so you couldn't be anywhere else in the world.

After a day pounding Prague's cobbled streets and sightseeing, head straight to the Augustine Spa and indulge in the aptly named Step into Heaven foot massage or a relaxing St. Thomas Beer Signature Body Treatment (apparently there are nourishing qualities to beer!) Following on the beer theme, start your evening with a drink in one of the hotel's

two quite distinctive bars. The 17th century St. Thomas Brewery Bar is housed in the original cellars where the monks used to brew their own St. Thomas Beer. Try the beer and you'll never drink a mass produced alternative again! Or enjoy one of the signature Angel's cocktails in the 18th century Lichfield Café & Bar, located in a beautiful barrel-vaulted hall complete with its own ceiling fresco where the Augustinian Monks' Refectory used to be.

Combine these unique experiences with an ambiance of warmth, impeccable service and charming staff and you can't fail to enjoy your stay at this incredible hotel.

MUSEUM **HOTEL**

Cappadocia / *Turkey*

Guests visiting the Museum Hotel in Cappadocia, Turkey, could be forgiven for thinking they have stepped into a time machine rather than straight off an airplane or out of a car. Set amidst old house ruins and ancient caves set in a sloping hill, the Museum Hotel enjoys some of the most sublime views of the valleys and mountains beyond. The entire hotel is designed to be a "living museum" as each room is decorated with antique furniture, handmade cushions, and real archaeological items. The Lil'a Restaurant serves modern and classic Turkish dishes with Anatolian and Cappadocian flavours. Take a magical trip on a hot air balloon for an unusual take of the surrounding natural wonders, or witness Anatolian Sufi traditions and watch the whirling dervishes. The Museum Hotel possesses a mystical aura that can't fail to transport you to a total state of serenity.

THE SOFA **HOTEL**
Istanbul / *Turkey*

Have you ever wished someone would deliver your favourite pasta dish in the middle of the night, or that much needed cocktail after a stressful afternoon conference call? At the Sofa Hotel in Istanbul, they offer a 24-hour "anything, anytime button" to ensure the highest quality of service.

This glamorous, artsy hotel allows its guests to sit back and be waited on in the middle of one of Istanbul's chicest neighbourhoods. Stroll through Nisantasi's chi-chi shops and gourmet restaurants; just walking distance from The Sofa. After shopping, the state-of-the-art spa and wellness center will leave you feeling utterly rejuvenated. The romantic ambience and five-star services simply cannot be topped.

On the top floor of The Sofa, the Frankie Istanbul restaurant offers fine, savoury Mediterranean dishes.

You will be searching for your "anything, anytime button" the moment you leave The Sofa, so why not stay an extra night?

ANASSA

Polis / *Cyprus*

Greek legend has it that Aphrodite, the goddess of love and beauty, arose from the rock (now named after her) just an hour's drive away from Anassa. Located at the foot of the Akamas and in close proximity to Aphrodite's Baths, these Mediterranean shores offer a divine setting for an exquisite hotel such as Anassa Hotel.

The location is not the only defining characteristic however. Guests are pampered like modern-day gods and goddesses and Anassa's personable staff is attentive to adults and children alike, promising an experience unhindered by daily annoyances.

Accommodation is flawless as well, with classic whitewashed exteriors that house Emperor-sized suites and villas, some with sea-facing terraces containing private plunge pools and whirlpools.

Diving, parasailing, wakeboarding, canoeing, windsurfing, and jet skiing are just a sprinkling of the water activities that are available, not to mention the wine-tastings and jeep safaris also accessible on the island.

For those looking for a day of relaxation and respite from the Mediterranean sun, the award-winning Anassa Thalassa Spa has an extensive assortment of therapies and treatments. In particular, the spa's various forms of thalassotherapy (a seawater therapy) should be tried to be believed.

Members are in for a culinary treat with four restaurants that offer an array of gastronomic menus which can accommodate those with food allergies and dietary restrictions. There are also dining options showcasing local flavours

in Anassa's 'Village Square' and a weekly beach barbeque, where a stunning sunset coupled with faint chords of a guitarist and bouzouki player create a heavenly ambiance.

ALMYRA

Paphos | *Cyprus*

When you arrive in Paphos, Cyprus you're immediately struck by the splendour of your surroundings. The Mediterranean sunshine and sea breeze provide a dazzling setting echoed by the notably warm welcome from the staff at the Almyra Hotel. There's an array of rooms and suites that overlook either Paphos harbour or lovely Mediterranean gardens – options are endless with dozens of different interconnecting rooms with both inland and sea views.

Almyra is mindful of all its guests no matter what their age or requirements. There are amenities and services for children and teens ranging from supervised clubs to a convenient "Baby Go Lightly" service (where you order all necessary items online before your departure). However, for those looking to escape the hustle and bustle of family life, the

Almyra restricts children to two of the four freshwater pools and other areas of the hotel, such as the Almyraspa and Eauzone Restaurant are also kid-free.

The renowned Almyraspa is a destination in itself, administering organic and marine-based therapies within its six treatment rooms, three spa suites, indoor pool and outdoor infinity pool areas. Additionally, Almyraspa's yoga deck, gym, tennis court and beauty salon enable members to rejuvenate mind, body and soul.

Almyra, meaning "taste of the sea," contains four major restaurants that showcase a variety of international and Mediterranean cuisines. Highly recommended: the Omakase, "trust the chef" menus, where guests can sample interesting Japanese-Mediterranean flavours.

Venture into the fishing town of Paphos and do take the time to visit the surrounding historical sights of Cyprus. Almyra's staff will gladly assist in transportation and reservations.

CONSTANTINOU BROS **ASIMINA SUITES HOTEL**

Paphos / Cyprus

If you're looking for rest and relaxation in serene beachfront surroundings then Asimina Suites Hotel ticks all the boxes. It's an adult only hotel – unique in Paphos – so there's no chance of the peace and tranquillity being shattered by over excited children!

From the moment you arrive, when you're ushered into a private check-in lounge and welcomed with cold towels, drinks and canapés, you'll feel like a VIP. Whilst relaxing on your padded sun lounger by the pool or in the manicured gardens, you can expect refreshing cold towels and complimentary fresh fruit to appear just as you're feeling warm or peckish, and at the raise of a hand a friendly, smiling staff member will be at your side with the drinks menu. Throughout your stay nothing is too much trouble but there's no constant harassment from over-zealous staff.

Add to this grown-up ambience the fact that there are no mass crowds (the hotel only has 119 suites), no pre-breakfast rush for sun beds (there's plenty to go around) and a heavenly Elixir spa, and now you're talking holiday! The Suites are luxuriously appointed with spacious marble bathrooms: treat yourself and book one of the seafront Executive Suites which boast their own private pool and Jacuzzi, as well as your own private beach cabana. You're spoilt for choice when it comes to dining, with four restaurants and two bars, but if you need to impress a loved one then you can't beat a romantic dinner as the sun sets at the Kymata beachfront restaurant.

DANAI BEACH **RESORT & VILLAS**

Sithonia / *Greece*

Perched up on the bluffs of the Aegean Peninsula, surrounded by beautiful Mediterranean gardens, Danai Beach Resort wins on looks alone. Overlooking an idyllic private beach dotted with white daybeds and umbrellas, the look and feel is utterly serene. The setting is matched by top-notch service and amenities for which the hotel has been rewarded as a member of the Leading Hotels of the World.

The suites and villas are adorned with outstanding art, sumptuous furniture and innovative design. Guests can enjoy a private swimming pool and a massage Jacuzzi bathtub in addition to 24-hour butler service.

There are four world-class restaurants and dining venues within the resort that specialize in Greek ,Mediterranean and French cuisine (courtesy of the renowned on-site Executive Chef de Cuisine); all graced with stunning views. Be sure to try The Sea Horse Grill and The Squirrel, or alternatively opt for private dining under the stars or by the sea.

33

GRACE **SANTORINI**

Imerovigli / *Greece*

As the most romantic hotel in one of the most romantic places on earth, the Grace Santorini delivers a rarefied level of indulgence. A boutique hotelier in the best sense of the word, every guest's stay is tailored to ensure an experience of consummate luxury. A glass of champagne and an icy towel to wash away the day's travel await your arrival, and each chic room is outfitted in stylishly minimalist pieces. For the ultimate Grace Santorini experience, book The Villa; equipped with its own private spa and pool, the suite is unbelievably exquisite. Positioned high above the Caldera, the hotel offers the perfect vantage point from which to enjoy the remarkable Santorini sunsets; dining al fresco is a must, beginning with a cocktail under the flaming sky, and ending with a starlit Tsipouro (the Grecian answer to Grappa). Revel in the infinity pool offering unrivalled views of the Aegean Sea, and cherish an unforgettable holiday.

34

AMAN **SVETI STEFAN**

Sveti Stefan / *Montenegro*

If you've seen a picture of Montenegro, (and fallen in love with it) chances are you've seen a picture of Sveti Stefan, a painfully pretty islet set in the azure Adriatic Sea. Following intensive renovation, Aman Sveti Stefan has opened its doors to welcome guests to an unforgettable experience of elegant indulgence. Wander through the quaintly cobbled lanes of the local village to discover a hidden courtyard down Poetry Lane (an authentic, charmingly-named location in Budva), or enjoy a leisurely lunch under the groves of olive trees. With six on-site private spa cottages, and an infinity pool set high in the cliffs overlooking the cerulean waters below, relaxation is guaranteed. The rooms are exquisitely sophisticated, with due attention paid to historically accurate details; the discerning guest will appreciate the rustically exposed stone walls, or the gorgeously domed ceilings. The pervading atmosphere is one of perfect calm, so take a second to breathe in one of the most beautiful corners of the world.

HOTEL **ARLBERG**

Lech / Austria

Hotel Arlberg is located in the heart of Lech and perfect as an intimate and luxury ski resort. This family run hotel makes you instantly feel as if you have just come home as soon as you walk through the front doors. Anyone who stays here will be privileged with both beautiful views of the surrounding area and amazing facilities.

The conveniently located slopes lead right back to the resort's front doors. In the summer you can enjoy all of the natural beauty the snow was covering—including sprawling meadows of lush grass and flowers.

Each of the rooms have their own décor and many guests find themselves choosing a specific room to come back and enjoy each time they visit. When you aren't on the slopes or relaxing

in your room, you can take time to visit the Senses Spa or lounge in the outdoor Jacuzzi.

Aside from skiing there are also other activities available to guests. During the summer season, car rallies are often held at Hotel Arlberg and Hannes Schneider, its owner, has an intense passion for cars that he enjoys sharing with guests. If you also have a keen interest in cars, or maybe just a desire to catch a glimpse of them close-up, then you will not be disappointed.

No matter when you visit Hotel Arlberg there will always be an adventure waiting for you. You can choose to ski through the resort, relax in the spa, go for a breathtaking hike along the Lech River or even indulge in classic car driving.

CARLTON HOTEL **ST MORITZ**

St Moritz / Switzerland

Do you dream of skiing down perfectly maintained trails fit for an Olympian in a glamorous and unspoilt setting? If so, the prestigious St. Moritz ski resort could be just the ticket.

Here, The Carlton Hotel offers impeccable customer service with the most breathtaking views, so prepare to be spoiled. Stepping out of the cold and into the lobby the welcome from the personal butlers is as warm as the roaring open fires and the cosy setting. Spacious suites, the finest spa in the valley and round-the-clock room service mean you can enjoy the evening and the apres-ski in true style.

386 square metres of walk-in wardrobe, kitchen, bedroom and 360 degree balcony views make up the Carlton Penthouse, where guests may soak in the bath or enjoy the walk-in shower in the opulence of the marble bathroom.

What's more, St. Moritz is located in an elegant, cosmopolitan area with world-class leisure activities, so non-skiers definitely don't have to worry about being stuck in the lodge all day!

A little dose of sophistication is par for the course at The Carlton Hotel St. Moritz.

PARK HYATT **ZURICH**

Zurich | Switzerland

Positioned in the heart of the city, the exclusive Park Hyatt Zurich is a sleek and sophisticated boutique hotel. Combining cool, cutting-edge design with a warm, welcoming ambiance, the hotel's location is unparalleled – just moments from the prestigious financial institutions of Paradeplatz Square, luxurious boutiques of Bahnhofstrasse and the scenic beauty of Lake Zurich.

The rooms channel a refined simplicity, incorporating an abundance of natural light. The bathrooms are appointed with rain showers and bespoke products from Parisian perfumer Blaise Mautin. Downstairs, guests gather around the open fireplace in The Lounge or sip cocktails at the stylish ONYX bar. Dinner is served in the Parkhuus Restaurant, renowned throughout Zurich as one of the city's premier gastronomic locations. Further indulgence comes from the Club Olympus spa, confirming the Park Hyatt Zurich as the ultimate destination for a relaxing city break.

GSTAAD **PALACE**

Gstaad / Switzerland

Picture yourself sitting next to a roaring fireplace sipping a delicious cocktail at the end of a day spent revelling in the splendour of the Swiss Alps. Too good to be true? Not as far as Gstaad Palace is concerned. Overlooking the majestic Swiss Alps, the Palace offers 104 beautifully decorated rooms and suites that all enjoy fantastic views. In particular, the luxurious President Suite located on the roof is spacious with three bedrooms and boasts a surrounding terrace complete with a Jacuzzi and sauna. Be sure to venture to the Walig Hut, a charming century-old farming hut that acts as a private hideaway high in the mountains. Its simplicity and serene surroundings make for a truly romantic setting.

The alpine spirit carries over into the Palace Spa, which offers a lavish hammam experience of two hours, composed of a seven-step relaxation programme. In addition to the five superb restaurants, guests are also encouraged to listen to live music at Le Bar du Grill. After sunset, The GreenGo nightclub is the place to be where the resident DJ Jim Leblanc gets the crowds in the party mood. Perhaps the hardest decision you will make while planning your fairy-tale vacation is whether to visit during the winter or summer months. Both are spectacularly beautiful but offer different activities ranging from skiing and snowboarding to paragliding and river rafting. In fact, why not do both?

GRAND HOTEL **BELLEVUE**

Gstaad | Switzerland

Glamorous and iconic, the Grand Hotel Bellevue is Gstaad's premier mountain resort. Forget the usual, twee pine interiors, this hotel is all about clean lines and understated elegance. Here a fresh, youthful design combines with all the grandeur and opulence you'd expect of an old-world hotel to create a classically contemporary feel.

Serenity, style and sophistication – this is the maxim by which the hotel operates. A home away from home, 57 generously proportioned rooms and suites offer stunning panoramas of the surrounding alpine scenery. Get even closer to the great outdoors and dine at the wonderfully rustic Le Petit Chalet. Set in the hotel's parklands, it serves traditional Swiss cheese dishes including tasty fondue and raclette. However, there's also high-end cuisine on offer at the Michelin-starred Prado Grill,

where Chef Urs Gschwend combines Mediterranean and Asian flavour to stunning gastronomic effect.

Sitting right at the very entrance of the charming, traffic free village of Gstaad, The Grand Hotel Bellevue is nestled in an idyllic park. Here, the mountains provide a diverse range of sports throughout the year, from glacier skiing and sledging in winter, to river rafting and paragliding in summer. After an active day, the Bellevue SPA is the perfect way to soothe tired muscles. A tranquil haven extending over more than 2,500sqm, this Asian-inspired spa is the ultimate holistic luxury retreat. Boasting a hammam, herbal steam baths, lanconium, salt and ice grotto and Finnish Sauna, the Bellevue SPA offers the complete detox experience in an oasis of exotic pampering.

GRAND HOTEL **LES TROIS ROIS**

Basel / Switzerland

One of Europe's oldest city hotels, the Grand Hotel Les Trois Rois is steeped in history. Napoleon, Pablo Picasso, Thomas Mann, Elizabeth II – the hotel's guest book reads like a chronicle of Europe's past. Yet it's not hard to see why this hotel receives such illustrious visitors. Situated in the very heart of Basel's scenic Old Town on the banks of the river Rhine, Les Trois Rois exudes old-world charm. Filled with precious antique furnishings and priceless pieces of art, the hotel captures the grandeur of the past through its luxurious aesthetic. Combine this with all the modern conveniences you'd expect of a five-star hotel and you're left with the perfect marriage of a classic yet contemporary retreat.

Indulge at the Chef Peter Knogl's sublime Cheval Blanc, the hotel's two Michelin-starred restaurant serving French haute cuisine. Or try Chez Donati,

a sophisticated Italian restaurant providing an alternative option for fine dining. Meanwhile Brasserie Les Trois Rois allows guests to savour an authentic taste of Switzerland through its creative local specialities. After dinner, enjoy a drink on the hotel's romantic terraces overlooking the Rhine or head to the Salon du Cigare for a good smoke. Not only does the lounge boast beautiful river views, it also offers a wide range of exceptional cigars, rare wines and single malts. It's an elegant way to unwind in this regal hotel.

Basel plays host to 40 museums making it the perfect destination for a cultural citybreak. Don't miss the Fondation Beyeler and the Vitra Design Museum, both of which are internationally renowned.

HOTEL **D'ANGLETERRE**

Geneva / *Switzerland*

Views captured from the Hotel d'Angleterre really are a joy to behold. Assuming its position opposite Lake Geneva, a marvel which tourists have been flocking to experience for centuries – see the example of Romantic poets Lord Byron and Percy Shelley -, it also takes in magnificent vistas of the Alps, crowned by snow-peaked Mont Blanc.

The hotel takes full advantage as it offers many rooms that employ the natural landscape as a backdrop. The 39 rooms and 6 suites come individually designed and vary their furnishings

to ensure that every one is a perfect fit for each guest's unique tastes. Some suites decked out in rich fabrics favour opulence, while others stay understated yet welcoming to focus on the spectacular landscape outside.

The fresh Alpine air promises to work wonders for any ailment, though if extra help is needed the hotel offers its own fitness centre, sauna, massage, reflexology and aromatherapy treatments. Rooms replete with original works of art really do make the hotel a home-from-

home. The exceptionally warm staff maintain a discreet but attentive service that undoubtedly contributes to the welcoming feel. Make the most of it – staff will even walk your dog if requested!

Come lunch or dinner time, Windows Restaurant is an excellent choice. The unobstructed views of Lake Geneva are particularly striking at sunset as the light dances on the water. Chef Philippe Audonnet serves up some of his favourite dishes that make the most of local produce and specialities as well as the international classics, with home-style dishes inspired by founder Bea Tollman. Highly esteemed French restaurant guide Gault Millau recognises the restaurant as among the best in Geneva. The impressive wine cellar is not to be missed and although the sheer choice can seem daunting, the sommelier carefully guides guests through the staggering selection. Take some time to experiment, making sure to select a new favourite which can be enjoyed back home to remind you of this magical moment.

Traditional afternoon tea is also served at the Windows Restaurant, where the century-old partnership with esteemed tea makers Betjeman and Barton is seriously professional – you'll discover teas you never knew existed or that you thought had long disappeared. Partnered with scones, jams and clotted cream, pastries, cakes and finger sandwiches, your diet may suffer a little but it's definitely worth it! Elsewhere, the Leopard Bar, named Hotel Bar of the Year by the Hideaway Guide, provides the cocktails, spirits and champagnes to make for an unforgettable night.

Once you've sampled all the hotel has to offer, take time to venture further afield. A ten-minute leisurely stroll takes you to the Rue du Rhone. Here lies a string of exclusive boutiques and restaurants, peppered with the finest jewellers and watchmakers you would expect from this part of the world. Boat trips that take in the wider area leave regularly from the quay opposite the hotel, though staff encourage guests to rent a car and take to the mountains to explore the Alpine landscape.

GRAND HOTEL **TREMEZZO**

Lake Como / *Italy*

Most striking amongst the wonders when visiting the Lake Como region are the endless and inimitable views. If you're looking to steal away with your loved one stop looking because Grand Hotel Tremezzo is it. For unobstructed views over the sparkling waters book a Rooftop Suite. The rooms are elegant and wonderfully spacious with panoramic terraces and Lake Como's only outdoor Jacuzzis- you'll feel like royalty.

The staff is the underlying strength of this wonderful establishment - they are utterly welcoming and will remember your name, your room number and make conversation with you every time they see you.

If Italy is renowned for its stunning land, it's also known for its universally loved cuisine. Be sure to reserve your table at La Terrazza to sample the menu courtesy of Gualtiero Marchesi, one of Italy's most influential gourmet chefs. There is nothing better than breakfast on the terrace overlooking Lake Como. For relaxation there are two sumptuous outdoor pools (one floating on the lake!) for lounging around. And if the surroundings need any further assistance in lulling you into a sense of luxurious oblivion there's the T Spa with indoor heated swimming pool (perfect for a swim overlooking the lake), Jacuzzis and exceptional pampering treatments.

The outcome is one of total peace and all this only a stone's throw away from the wonders of the legendary Villa Carlotta next door and the little villages beyond along the lake shores. The perfect romantic getaway with all the glamour of a James Bond film and double the class.

45

HOTEL **CASTELLO DI CASOLE**
Casole d'Elsa | Italy

Situated in an historic castle dating back to the
10th century, guests arrive at the Hotel Castello
di Casole in Tuscany along a cypress-lined lane
that leads to an elegant courtyard. The estate
produces its own wine and olive oil, offering
tastings as well as cooking, pottery, and language
lessons. Rustic food is prepared in the classic
Italian tradition, including handmade pastas, fresh
organic vegetables, fresh fish and game all paired
with fine Italian wines. The estate is also a Model
Game Reserve for its thriving vegetation and animal
populations, and guests are encouraged to hunt
and hike through the grounds. The estate's original
wine cellar has been restored into the Essere Spa,
which provides some excellent health and beauty
treatments. This luxurious Tuscan getaway – part of
the illustrious Timbers Resorts Hotel & Residences
group - is the epitome of romance; tucked away
in the picture perfect Italian countryside.

CASTIGLION **DEL BOSCO**

Tuscany / *Italy*

Castiglion del Bosco, set in the rolling hills of southern Tuscany, is the ideal place to immerse yourself in rural Italian culture. Wine-tasting sessions are available and feature the estate's produce, the renowned Brunello di Montalcino, along with stores of the finest French vintages.

At the centre of Il Borgo, the lovingly restored 18th century village that now houses the estate lies the priest's house. Here La Canonica Cooking School teaches guests to create genuine Tuscan dishes that can be easily brought home and shown off to appreciative friends and family.

Ristorante Campo Del Drago sources much of its ingredients from the Orto organic garden, which provides over 180 varieties of vegetables and herbs, so you know you're getting the authentic Tuscan experience. The closed cycle means you feel a real sense of inclusion – and makes the food taste twice as good!

There are an abundance of pleasant distractions with which to pass time, all within the estate's grounds. The 18-hole private golf course designed by world-renowned British Open champion Tom Weiskopf is worked into the contours of the spectacular landscape.

Aside from offering truffle-hunting expeditions and a wide variety of sporting activities, landscape painting classes are a great way to capture the feeling of your holiday in a lasting memento.

Daniela Steiner's Care Suite Spa is a centrepiece of the estate. It offers unconventional techniques that make use of the area's organic produce to leave you feeling fresh and ready to embrace all the area has to offer. A hike or bike ride along the sloping hills for example!

IL **PELLICANO**

Grosseto / *Italy*

If you want the intimacy of your home paired with unrivalled splendour and dedicated staff working to fulfil your individual needs and desires, then look no further than the exclusive Il Pellicano. What started off in 1965 with just 18 guestrooms has grown to 50 rooms and suites and six cottages spread over 17 acres, yet has still managed to retain the effortless sophistication and special atmosphere that is the heart and soul of the hotel.

Il Pellicano provides you with all the resources necessary to make your stay unforgettable. Treat yourself to a luxury massage at the Pelliclub; take a one of a kind cooking course with the hotel's Michelin star chef; swim in the heated saltwater pool, or spend the day island-hopping on one of the hotels' boats. With former guests including Charlie Chaplin and Gianni Agnelli you're in good company.

CAESAR **AUGUSTUS**

Anacapri / Italy

'Hotel' may be the wrong word for this heavenly retreat set high in the cliffs on Capri above the urban sprawl beneath: it implies something commonplace, detached. Staying at the Caesar Augustus is more like swanning into the Italian home of a wildly wealthy aunt, Gatsby-esque in her generosity and motherly in her warmth and affection. Coming up the lantern-lined cobbled drive (preferably by moonlight), an enchanting spell falls over you as you enter the grounds; so this is where peacefulness has been hiding...

A word of warning, then: leaving this idyllic mansion will prove harder than most. The terrace's unparalleled 360° panoramic views of the Golfo di Napoli, encompassing the somnolent Mount Vesuvius, Sorrento, and the Amalfi Coast, are a major draw for tourists and locals alike. At night,

groups gather on the gorgeous veranda to enjoy a glass of wine while watching the sky melt into indigo over the horizon, the stars mere diamante pinpricks in the velvety firmament. Wake up late every morning to a cappuccino in bed, and wander downstairs for a dip in the infinity pool overlooking the azure ocean before indulging in a massage al fresco.

Capri itself is enchantingly picturesque and provides fodder for many day trips; wander around the tiny lanes before happening upon a hidden piazza and café for a bite to eat, or embark on a more athletic venture around the island's rugged mountainous terrain. The restaurant at the Caesar Augustus provides the perfect epicurean end to each day; enjoy freshly baked focaccia and olives before trying their toothsome fresh pasta made in-house every day, paired with a bottle

of Campanian Primitivo. Complimentary tissues provided for the odd tear or two upon departure.

HOTEL **DANIELI**
Venice / *Italy*

If Italy is arguably the origin of opulence, then Venice is the well from which it sprang. Of all the stunning Venetian locales, the Hotel Danieli best epitomizes a typically unapologetic lavishness. Built in the 14th century for the Dandolos, a noble Venetian family, the Hotel Danieli has maintained its aura of regal luxury throughout the centuries. As you walk through the ancient wooden doors the scene is breathtaking. Lustrous marble floors cover the expanse of the reception, while pink marble columns reach up to the intricately carved, golden ceilings. Riotous bursts of flowers tumble from intricate urns, as original Murano glass chandeliers sparkle overhead.

The rooms are similarly splendid; for an extraordinary experience, book the jewel-like Royal Suite. Evoking Venice under the reign of the Doge Dandolo in 1192, the suite is swathed in golden tapestries, and bedecked in glittering crystal. Equally stunning are the three Signature suites designed by Pierre Yves-Rochon; drawing inspiration from three timeless beauties (the silver-screen siren Greta Garbo, the operatic diva Maria Callas, and the ethereal Princess Grace of Monaco), the suites are trimmed in elegantly sophisticated dove greys, soft bronzes, and pistachio greens, and are perfectly reminiscent of the eternal style of these women.

Sip a glass of Prosecco on the rooftop Terrazza Danieli, the Italian sunset staining the sky behind the Palazzo Ducale. The Hotel is ideally located on the Riva degli Schiavoni to provide easy access to the surrounding cultural attractions, including la Biennale di Venezia. For an appropriately luxurious end to your stay, take a wooden speedboat to the airport - we promise you won't miss the traffic.

HOTEL **GRITTI PALACE**

Venice / Italy

This iconic palazzo, recently restored by Donghia Design, is secreted in a peaceful Venetian neighbourhood. A leisurely stroll heading towards the Piazza San Marco leads you past designer boutiques, antique dealers and artisan workshops and is a great way to spend a sunny afternoon. Within easy reach are the Peggy Guggenheim Collection, the Punta della Dogana and La Fenice Opera House meaning there is no excuse not to return home suitably cultured.

The Gritti Palace itself offers views that stretch from San Giorgio Island to the strikingly beautiful Santa Maria della Salute church, taking in the Accademia in the process. People have gathered for almost six centuries to sample the palazzo's delights and one of our particular favourite haunts has always been the Club Dei Doge

restaurant, from whose terrace guests can look down on The Grand Canal. Its 'casual chic' atmosphere by day transitions to formal dining come evening, and it is after the sun sets that the spectacular views really are at their best.

Bar Longhi also makes use of the Gritti Palace's canal side location, with the terrace's dedicated barman ready to serve signature drinks or even develop cocktails with new twists. The soufflé dessert speciality served up deserves consideration. Whatever your choice, it is sure to be served up in style – accompanied either by canal views or Pietro Longhi paintings that adorn the bar's interior walls.

English novelist W Somerset Maugham remarked on the way the Gritti Palace guest

can return to the same seat year after year to feel like a member of the family. You get the sense this stands to be true today.

HOTEL **D'INGHILTERRA**

Rome / Italy

Once the aristocratic residence of 16th century Princes of Torlonia, the Hotel D'Inghilterra has continually served the international elite for centuries. Located moments away from the famous Spanish Steps and in the heart of the fashion district, the Hotel D'Inghilterra is the ideal hotel for those wanting to explore the rich history of the city and also its modern pleasures.

English poets Byron, Keats, and Shelley of the 1800s and American authors Mark Twain and Hemingway of the 1900s chose the Hotel D'Inghilterra for its sense of privacy and refinery, and the tradition continues today with 88 room and suite options. Each room and suite has its own individual design and offers the luxurious comfort of a private noble residence. In particular, the Presidential Suite is a spectacular experience as it promises one of the best views of the

unbelievable panorama of the Eternal City. Situated on the top floor, the Presidential Suite Roof Garden is perfect for any private events and the spacious interior is beautifully decorated with antique art.

At the Café Romano, Chef Antonio Vitale fuses simplicity, extraordinary ingredients, and creativity to bring his guests a unique take on Roma cuisine. Go to the Café Romano to enjoy a delicious buffet breakfast, a luncheon with friends, a snack before shopping, or a candlelit dinner. The Bond Bar, with its leather armchairs and vintage furniture and art, also has a variety of cocktails and serves some of the best coffee in Rome.

The fascinating history and splendour of the Hotel d'Inghilterra echoes the city's greatness and as they say, when in Rome…

53

LA POSTA **VECCHIA**

Rome / Italy

Imagine cradling a wine glass in your hand as you take in the spectacular sea view from the terrace. The sun is beginning to set and it's almost time for dinner. Instead of dining in the hotel's Michelin star restaurant, The Cesar, tonight you have reservations for a private dinner. Instead of a table in the garden gazebo, you've chosen to have your meal served by candlelight in the hotel's private Ancient Roman artefacts museum. This image is just one reason why discerning guests return time and again to La Posta Vecchia Hotel.

Once the summer residence of Roman emperors this 17th century villa is now an exclusive resort. The guestrooms reflect the hotel's sense of timeless elegance, combining antique furniture with contemporary amenities. Swim in the indoor pool overlooking the sea or head to the private beach; cycle along the coastal path or

indulge in a spa treatment. If you have ever wanted to experience a time of refined splendour and grandeur, this intimate hotel should be on top of your list for your next holiday.

MASSERIA **SAN DOMENICO**

Brindisi / Italy

If you are looking to escape your busy life for a holiday in a traditionally elegant Italian resort then Masseria San Domenico should be top of your list of places to visit. Located in Italy's Puglia region, this hotel is a tasteful renovation of a 15th century watchtower set in acres of olive trees.

This extraordinary setting makes for a happy marriage- a boutique style hotel with first-class facilities in a natural, rustic environment. There are of course two outdoor pools, a Thalassotherapy spa and private beach area, but there are also tennis courts, a gym, and an 18-hole golf course for a spot of action.

Gourmets are in for a treat – top-class, home-grown culinary fare from the local region of Puglia is a highlight at San Domenico. Evenings are cosy in the Ulivo Bar, complete with fireplace and even a humidor and separate area for cigar enthusiasts.

Recently opened, the extraordinary 'San Domenico a Mare' boasts four beautiful rooms as close to the beach as you can get, with accompanying seafood restaurant, La nassa, providing fine dining.

Masseria San Domenico has all the makings of the ultimate romantic getaway for couples.

55

GRAND HOTEL **DU CAP-FERRAT**

Saint Jean Cap-Ferrat / *France*

The Grand Hotel du Cap-Ferrat delivers a dose of refined, self-assured luxury that is increasingly rare in today's flashy world of ostentation. Established over a century ago in this naturally beautiful corner of France, the Grand Hotel has played host to many interesting characters throughout its illustrious existence, including artists like Charles Boyer and Jacques Thibaud. It's no wonder, then, that the hotel is well-versed in chic, understated opulence.

The hotel is nestled like a pearl in 17 acres of lush forests. Days here are sunny with the aroma of sea salt and clementines pervading the airy halls and suites. Sip a French martini in the all-white hotel bar under the lime green Murano chandeliers for a break from the sun, or take a ramble in the Jean Mus-designed gardens. The Spa was recently voted one of 2012's best destination spas, and offers treatments from top brands such as Bellefontaine, Carita and Emmanuel Levain. We suggest packing your dreamiest kaftan for pool-side lounging and to accommodate the surfeit induced by Executive Chef Didier Aniès' Michelin-starred restaurant. Dine on Aquitaine caviar and baby leek lasagne under the Aleppo pines and enjoy one of the world's best wine collections, including over 150 vintage bottles from Château d'Yquem and 141 rare bottles of Sauternes, (that can be, or rather. should be reserved for private dinners and tastings).

To cater to those seeking total seclusion, the gorgeous Villa Rose Pierre, a private 4-bedroom mansion is available for lettings and comes complete with a private gym, pool, tennis courts, and dedicated staff. Parfait.

HOTEL **ROYAL-RIVIERA**

Saint Jean Cap Ferrat / **France**

"I can resist everything except temptation". Never did Oscar Wilde's legendary quote ring truer than here, driving along the scenic Basse Corniche, drawing up in front of Hotel Royal-Riviera and catching a glimpse of the glorious gardens inspired by the great wordsmith himself. Being here would go down as one of life's most memorable moments. Set atop the Peninsula of Cap Ferrat flirting with the edges of Beaulieu, Nice and Monaco, the five-star hotel takes centre stage in the most exclusive of locations. It's the only luxury property in the region to enjoy its own private sandy beach and if you dream of staying in an intimate private Mediterranean villa complete with the glamour of a palace, then dream no more! As you set down your bags in one of the 94 impeccable rooms and, suites, throw open the windows and breathe in the warm, fragrant air, you immediately feel the shackles of time slipping away. As expected, the dining is exquisite at The Panorama where flavours of Provence bring sunshine to your plate. Like coming home, Royal-Riviera encourages lounging on your sea-facing balcony, reading a book in the gardens and taking in the sounds of nature without a care in the world and in utter comfort and privacy. Entrust any requests and special services to the exclusive concierge for that extra touch of personal service. Like the breath-taking views, the gorgeous Villa Kerylos and the sea breeze, the feelings of contentment here are priceless, lodging firmly in your memory bank for a lifetime.

CHÂTEAU DE **BAGNOLS**

Bagnols / *France*

The Beaujolais countryside is known world-wide for its beauty: Vineyards, forests and rolling hills are already firmly set in the France of our imagination. Visitors will find the Château de Bagnols fits happily with the discerning guest's high expectations of a rural French retreat.

The hotel prides itself on being the finest five-star deluxe Château hotel in France, down largely to the loving restoration by Lady Hamelin after its discovery as a derelict property as recently as 1987. The Renaissance wall and ceiling paintings subsequently revealed tell the story of a time when nearby Lyon was among the finest Renaissance cities in Europe.

Original features complement the atmosphere perfectly, meaning visitors really do feel a part of the Château de Bagnols' considerable history. Set alongside the original 13th-century dry moat and incorporating a drawbridge as the entrance, a visit here is a lesson in the art of escapism.

The Salle des Gardes restaurant reaps the benefits of the château's location, with locally sourced ingredients making up many of the dishes available on the menu. The wealth of stellar regional produce used means every meal captures the spirit of the region. Beaujolais charcuterie, river fish and cheeses are partnered with specially designed china, glass and linen that evoke the hotel's Renaissance grandeur. Food is served in the opulent dining room, where you'll be eating like a king – Charles VIII's visit in 1490 is commemorated with a coat of arms above the grand Gothic fireplace. The accompanying outdoor terrace is flanked by century-old lime trees with leaves that flutter in the summer breeze to soundtrack your Beaujolais meal.

Many of the 19 apartments at the Château de Bagnols are decorated with Renaissance wall and ceiling frescoes, though guests will quickly discover that a wealth of history does not come at the expense of comfort. The plush furnishings embellish the feeling of intimacy that pervades each apartment. It is well worth planning a night spent in the confines of your room if only to indulge in the sheer splendour of four-poster beds and room service.

There are a host of ways to stay entertained throughout a visit; our particular highlight being the French gardens where guests wander through picturesque vineyards. Wine tastings, hot-air balloon flights, and even horse carriage rides are on offer, with each providing great ways to capture the essence of an unforgettable stay in the Beaujolais countryside.

LES SUITES DE LA **POTINIÈRE**
Courchevel / France

Les Suites de la Potinière nestled in the French Alps in Courchevel is a little like a James Bond hideaway - a destination that has become synonymous with alpine glamour both on and off the slopes and which has attracted the jet-set for the past 40-plus years.

Les Suites de la Potinière stands at the foot of the mountains with easy access to over 370 miles of ski slopes. You can even take a break between runs to luge or toboggan down the mountains. The ski runs are nice and wide and accommodate all levels of skiers so don't worry if you usually stick to the bunny slope! In the cosy warmth of the hotel, the bar and lounge deliver a twist on the typical ski glamorous lodge with a psychedelic theme of décor (think love and peace signs on the wall) as guests relax and sip wine and champagne. In fact nothing is ordinary here in Les Suites and no detail is left to chance: don't be surprised to see a ski butler appear before you to help you take off your ski boots. (How about that for service?) A ski room with boot warmers is also a

much-needed pleasure and well-thought out after an icy day on the mountain—there is nothing worse than putting on a cold, wet boot in the morning! For fans of the après-ski scene there is plenty of choice as the hotel is within walking distance of Courchevel's restaurants, bars and elegant boutiques.

The guest rooms are dressed in warm shades of red and brown with soft and silky fabrics to keep you toasty. The exclusive suites (numbering only fifteen, plus the 450sqm Penthouse Apartment) are spacious and feature all the mod-cons like Wi-Fi, plasma screen televisions and music systems. Some may fancy a massage or a work-out to stretch after hours of skiing and the state-of-the-art fitness and spa are well-equipped for any injury or need with a team of professionals whose life-work is dedicated to making guests feel good. There's even an indoor swimming pool -surrounded by candles - for an extra touch of romance. Seasoned guests will know (but may well keep it secret) that the hotel's penthouse

complete with magnificent fireplace, commands the most breath-taking views over the Alps.

Gourmets are in for a treat with fabulous comfort food: French and English cuisine in-house as well as on the room service menu. Perfect for unwinding at the end of a day in winter wonderland.

TRIANON PALACE **VERSAILLES**

Versailles / *France*

When you check in at the Trianon Palace Versailles you are entering a world of refinement and modernity. This exceptional woodland retreat is located near the Tranquil Royal Domain, the romantic city of Paris, and the Palace of Versailles. This Waldorf Astoria hotel is a symbol of luxury at the heart of one of the most historically prestigious places in the world.

The Trianon Palace features 199 elegant guest rooms designed by Fiona Thompson who combined the finest of traditional Grand Siècle design and contemporary opulence so that each room feels like an oasis. The bathrooms are spacious and beautifully ornamented with mosaic tiles, creating a miniature spa within each suite.

There is the luxury Spa Guerlain, dedicated to providing each guest with the best in well-

being and beauty. For your dining experiences at the Trianon Palace we highly recommend the traditional French cuisine prepared at the Gordon Ramsey au Trianon. If you are looking for a wider food selection and an immensely diverse wine list, La Veranda is equally exceptional.

For families and couples alike, this is the perfect destination to explore the beauty of Versailles and Paris. You can take a stroll through the three-acre wooded park or just enjoy a day relaxing in your room and the spa. Either way, the Trianon Palace has been considered one of Europe's grandest destinations since 1910.

SHANGRI-LA **HOTEL PARIS**

Paris / France

The French place great importance on living the good life and the Shangri-La Hotel, Paris encapsulates this approach in all respects. The hotel's old-world elegance has remained since its time as the home of Napoleon Bonaparte's grand-nephew, Prince Roland Bonaparte.

The world famous Shangri-La hospitality and the Asian values embraced by all of the hotels are undeniable – you'll be treated like royalty from the minute you arrive. The hotel has 81 spectacular rooms and suites that are decorated in soothing shades of blue, white and ecru, in keeping with both European Empire and Asian aesthetics.

Rooms with a view of the Eiffel Tower are particularly recommended for their "wow factor".

There's a diverse range of award-winning restaurants featuring French and Asian cuisine. L'Abeille, the hotel's French gourmet restaurant, promises guests an unparalleled gastronomic experience as it received two Michelin stars in the Michelin Guide 2012. Shang Palace is home to authentic Cantonese cuisine for the first time ever in Paris.

You can plan unforgettable private events in the hotel's historical function rooms, whose architecture and history are such that two-thirds are registered under the protection of the French monuments historiques.

Shangri-La Hotel, Paris is centrally located in the 16th district of Paris, just minutes from the Place des Etats-Unis, the Place d'Iéna and the Place du Trocadero, on the Chaillot Hill. The Triangle d'Or, the Champs-Elysées, and a myriad of luxury boutiques and museums are also just a stone's throw away.

Let's just say that never again will you wonder where to stay in the City of Lights.

LE **BURGUNDY**

Paris / *France*

Le Burgundy Paris is an ode to good of living. Oozing lightness and sophistication, the hotel is quintessentially Parisian with chic décor and understated elegance. It's the ultimate in contemporary luxury, playing on the natural light which drenches the bright rooms and modern interiors. It is also fantastically located, sitting right in the heart of Paris on the prestigious Rue Saint Honoré. Yet Le Burgundy is intimate despite being in the middle of the hustle and bustle outside. Perfect then as a base for trips to the neighbouring shopping destinations, with some of the biggest names in fashion only minutes away. What's more, Le Spa Burgundy provides the ideal post-retail therapy relaxation, with revitalizing pedicures to calm tired feet and soothing massages for those aching shoulders.

Once you're restored, make sure you don't miss the exclusive Le Baudelaire restaurant for dinner. The Michelin-starred restaurant has a fresh approach and holds some wonderful surprises in store for any self-respecting gourmet. The menu features some Parisian culinary classics that are given an international twist. The pastry chef's creations served in the beautiful Winter Garden are worth saving yourself for but whatever you opt for, one thing is certain - the service will be impeccable.

It's friendly and efficient, lending warmth to what is undoubtedly a very cool hotel. Guests are treated like VIPs and tend to return time and again, which is why Le Burgundy feels like a home-from-home.

LE BRISTOL **PARIS**

Paris / *France*

Deep in the Parisian heartland of fashion boutiques and galleries along the Rue du Faubourg Saint-Honoré, Le Bristol Paris has plenty by way of pleasant distractions. But with guestrooms among the largest in the city vaunting sumptuous fabrics and lavish bathrooms why would you want to leave?

The sixth floor rooftop swimming pool with neighbouring sunbathing area provides spectacular views of leafy streets and is a particular highlight. Another is the Epicure restaurant which boasts the services of three-Michelin-starred chef Eric Frechon. The Spa Le Bristol by La Prairie boasts treatments which are sure to relax even the tightest muscles, and this is in no small part owing to the Spa's impressive new design.

Guests enjoying the hotel's hospitality will be in good company. Throughout the 20th century illustrious guests included Charlie Chaplin, Rita Hayworth and Grace Kelly. Carry on the tradition with 'Fashion High Teas' on Saturdays or wine tasting on Mondays.

MANDARIN ORIENTAL **PARIS**

Paris | France

Food, fashion, culture - Mandarin Oriental, Paris encompasses all the ingredients for the perfect Parisian break. Situated in the very heart of Paris on the prestigious rue Saint Honoré, the hotel's location is truly unbeatable. Rubbing shoulders with the capital's top fashion houses, the hotel is also just moments away from the cultural hotspots of the Louvre, Musée d'Orsay and Tuileries gardens. Yet it's what's within this exceptional hotel which really stands out.

Step inside from the bustling street and you're met with an oasis of calm. Here, contemporary French design is given an oriental twist to create sumptuous surroundings. Walk through the lobby to the hotel's beautiful gardens and you'll be greeted with views stretching across the capital's landmarks. Boasting some of the most spacious guest rooms in Paris, suites feel more like private apartments at this prestigious address. The jewel in the hotel's crown is undoubtedly the Royale

Mandarin Suite – an opulent two-bedroom suite complete with private dining room, personal gym and terrace with fabulous views of the Eiffel Tower.

It wouldn't be Paris without wonderful food and Mandarin Oriental, Paris has it in abundance. Under the gastronomic guidance of its esteemed culinary director, the hotel's signature restaurant, Sur Mesure par Thierry Marx, has been awarded two Michelin stars. Cool, white walls provide the perfect blank canvas for Marx's innovative cuisine, whilst the interiors pay homage to Parisian haute couture. The capital's fashionable roots are also apparent at Mandarin Oriental, Paris's other restaurant, Camélia. Drawing its name from Chanel's floral emblem, tables spill out onto the landscaped courtyard as guests are served contemporary French fare amongst the garden's camellias.

For cocktails, Bar 8 is the ideal rendezvous. The dramatic marble bar, quarried in Spain and sculpted

in Italy, provides the centrepiece for this stylish venue. With tiny lights dotted across the low tables and Lalique crystals inlaid into the wooden walls, the whole bar quite literally sparkles. Equally dazzling is The Spa at Mandarin Oriental, Paris; a serene oasis where highly professional therapists deliver world-renowned holistic treatments. Here, the emphasis is on pure relaxation, with private couple spa suites offering private vitality pools. Yet when the hotel itself is so blissfully serene, a zen-like state is guaranteed during your stay anyway.

Don't miss Mandarin Oriental's signature Cake Shop. Serving delicious sweet and savoury delicacies, the famous Le Saint-Honoré puff pastry, filled with vanilla cream and caramel is sublime.

LE MEURICE

Paris / France

Le Meurice has welcomed some of the most illustrious figures in history from Queen Victoria to Tchaikovsky, and has hosted such glittering events as Picasso's wedding dinner and Coco Chanel's glittering receptions. Sitting across from the Tuileries Garden and only steps away from Place Vendôme and Rue Saint-Honoré, Le Meurice's magical setting and enchanting history has captured the hearts of many passing through Paris over the past 190 years.

The magnificent décor of the hotel mirrors the grandeur of the Grand Siècle, with recent surrealist style restorations by Philippe Starck. The 160 rooms and suites are reminiscent of 18th century Parisian homes and feature a plethora of contemporary luxuries. The Restaurant Le Meurice is centrepiece with the gourmet Parisian creations of Yannick Alléno, the three Michelin-star chef. Le Meurice is a source of inspiration for those captivated by the heritage, culture and style of the City of Light and has transformed the luxury hotel experience into a fine art.

PINE CLIFFS **TERRACES & VILLAS**
Algarve / *Portugal*

Pine Cliffs Terraces & Villas in the Algarve is the perfect destination for a vacation that combines the complete privacy of a villa or terrace with the amenities of a hotel resort, such as 24-hour room service and daily housekeeping. The modern décor, warm colours, and impeccably manicured grounds make for a luxurious, boutique style setting with the privacy of home.

Each of the four-bedroom villas is perfect for larger groups and is surrounded by a golf course, swimming pool, tennis courts, and picturesque gardens. The terraces are all stunningly appointed and boast lush gardens - combining the best of nature and design.

A bonus is guest access to all of the amenities of the resort, including the sun beds, restaurants on the grounds, and the spa. In addition, Pine Cliffs

Resort offers a tennis academy, country club, and Kids' Club that are reserved solely for their guests.

SHA **WELLNESS CLINIC**

Alicante / *Spain*

Situated in Albair Beach is the SHA Wellness Clinic. This is a stunningly modern and beautiful destination for anyone in need of some thorough physical and mental rejuvenation. Part of the Sierra Helada National Park, it sits perched on the mountainside with priceless views of the Mediterranean Sea. Comfortable temperatures are guaranteed year round and the World Health Organization has noted it as having the world's best climate.

Ultra-professional (and personable) SHA staff combine the ideals of ancient oriental

techniques with the advanced western medicine. Expect to be treated to some of the most cutting-edge, rejuvenating and relaxing treatments you will ever experience.

Aside from holistic massages and facials, a clean, Zen approach to life is the underlying theme at SHA. Take advantage of the nutritional advice on offer and for that extra special touch, opt for a personalized menu of treatments for the ultimate health kick.

HOTEL **HACIENDA NA XAMENA**

Ibiza | Spain

The first question that comes into your head as you wind your way further up the hill on your way to the Hotel Hacienda Na Xamena is: "when are we going to stop?" You're high above sea level here, 180 metres high to be precise, but it's only when you are ushered through the great Ibicencan finca that its situation dawns on you. This gem of hotel is quite literally carved into and perched on the cliff top overlooking the most breathtaking view of the Mediterranean you could possibly ask for. Framed by pine trees leaning into the wind, the white walls of this impossibly chic yet rustic hacienda-style

hotel positively glimmer in the sunlight. So you've arrived in what can only be described as your own corner of heaven- away from any stress, noise or pollution and the calming effect is palpable from the moment you step out of the car. (We defy anyone to reach this place on foot, so if remote getaways are your thing you've come to the right place).

The location and history lend a particular character to the hotel. In the late 60s, Ibiza was even more isolated than it is today and Daniel Lipszyc, a Belgian architect, and his wife were among those

who fell in love with the island. They undertook its construction with a view to maintaining and protecting the natural beauty of its surroundings.

There are 70 rooms and suites each with spectacular sea views and Jacuzzi next to the panoramic window. There are three different ambiances depending on the level of luxury you're seeking and the theme continues throughout with a memorable Thalasso therapy spa set into the cliff - Cascadas Suspendidas - a labyrinth of whirlpools of varying heat and intensity designed to work the muscles and enhance circulation as you overlook the sea. For massage and well being treatments the spa La Posidonia is a haven of peace with private cabins outdoors and in for relaxation.

It's a treat to sit and take in the naturally beautiful surroundings on the terrace of Las Cascadas as you breakfast next to the pool or enjoy a romantic dinner at El Eden Restaurant or Sueño de Estrellas - a symphony of twinkling lights and gourmet Mediterranean cuisine.

Cooking, boat trips, live music, DJ performances and a chill-out music lounge add to the laid-back glamour and fun at this most extraordinary and authentic Ibencan retreat. Just don't tell everyone about it because you really will want to keep this secret to yourself.

FINCA **CORTESIN**
Malaga / Spain

This oasis of tranquillity, ideally located between Marbella and Sotogrande in the seductive south of Spain, was designed to engage and enchant every sense. Bathed in golden Mediterranean sunshine, the quotidian worries of everyday life are sloughed off as soon as you enter the cobbled drive of Finca Cortesin. Enjoy panoramic ocean or mountain views from your lush four-poster bed as you breakfast on fresh pastry, adjusting to the indulgently unhurried pace of this resort. Cool down each day by taking a dip in the sparkling, Olympic-scaled pool; or if you're in one of the villas, enjoy the privacy of your own personal pool (bathing suits optional). With five separate, exquisite restaurants, choices abound for the gourmands. Particularly alluring is the Beach Club restaurant, with distinctly Mediterranean offerings available overlooking the sparkling infinity pool. Recline in Balinese sunbeds surrounded by fine gardens while sipping a cocktail.

Ready to tee off? The emerald-hued greens await your arrival, and the course plays host to the Volvo World Match Play Championship. For those otherwise inclined, the world-famous spa, an airy, light-filled dream, is absolutely not to be missed.

CONTENTS AFRICA, MIDDLE EAST & INDIAN OCEAN

ARMANI **HOTEL DUBAI**

Dubai | United Arab Emirates

Armani Hotel Dubai is the first hotel designed by Giorgio Armani and is the epitome of style and taste. The fashion designer has brought the essence of Italian chic to this hotel housed in the world's tallest building Burj Khalifa, soaring above downtown Dubai with commanding views of the city and its glittering skyline. Guests here are treated to a veritable lifestyle experience with aesthetically stunning signature suites and rooms; a broadly excellent choice of seven innovative restaurants; exclusive boutiques, the first in-hotel Armani/SPA and, crucially, a

team of round the clock Lifestyle Managers - part of the 'Stay with Armani' philosophy that ensures a 'home-away-from-home' experience. The Armani Hotels & Resorts strongly believe that travel is as much an emotional journey as a physical one and as a result each hotel guest is lucky enough to be assigned a personal Lifestyle Manager. Think of this as personal contact and host from the moment you book your room to the checking out and beyond. Nothing is too much trouble...You need someone to give you the best addresses in Dubai, fix you a meal in the middle

of the night or take care of your laundry - no worries, it's all taken care of in the blink of an eye!

This hotel is so much more than a luxurious, stylish and elegant holiday and business destination - it has been meticulously designed and laid out by Giorgio Armani himself with the guest's comfort in mind at all times. This means that every detail, from the bespoke furnishings to the restaurant menus and in-room amenities are the fruit of painstaking planning and an appreciation for the guest's emotional reaction. The plan has been plainly successful as

you will agree reclining on your king sized bed and looking out at the uninterrupted view of the landmark The Dubai Fountain outside your window.

The seven hotel restaurants cater to all manner of tastes and include a selection of world cuisines ranging from Japanese and Indian to Mediterranean and authentic Italian fine dining. Also popular among guests are the three exclusive retail outlets: Armani/Galleria, the first and only place in Dubai where the Giorgio Armani/Privé collection is showcased; Armani/Dolci, a luxurious confectionary store offering a selection of chocolates, and more; and Armani/Fiori, a floral boutique offering exquisite fresh flower arrangements and exclusively designed vases by Giorgio Armani.

Relaxation and pampering the senses are taken very seriously here too and as a result, the hotel has introduced the Armani/SPA that offers fully tailored sensory experiences that suit individual needs. Each unique space in the Armani/SPA provides a context for personalised treatments, personal fitness and sequential thermal bathing, as well as for private and social relaxation.

Downtown Dubai, described as "The Centre of Now" is the place to be, with the hotel just walking distance from The Dubai Mall, the world's largest shopping and entertainment destination. But the chances are you won't stray too far from the serenity of Armani Hotel Dubai...

AL MAHA DESERT **RESORT & SPA**

Dubai / *United Arab Emirates*

Each suite in Al Maha Desert Resort comes complete with wooden deck overlooking the desert and private swimming pool. Designed to resemble a Bedouin camp and furnished with authentic regional artefacts it really does feel as if the room blends seamlessly with the landscape.

It is perfectly reasonable to expect to catch sight of some spectacular wildlife, with the resort at the heart of the Dubai Desert Conservation Reserve, which offers a haven for indigenous Arabian mammals and birds. The infinity pool is a great point from which to sneak a glimpse.

What we really encourage, though, is to take up the offer of two complimentary desert activities per night's stay and properly engage with the desert landscape. We found the Camel Rides a particular highlight, allowing for a champagne stop on the dunes mid-ride.

Gastronomy is at its peak at Al Maha with the finest cuisine on offer in exquisite settings. Dine in style at the signature Al Diwaan Restaurant, experience dining under the Arabian sky at night with Dune Dining or relax with a romantic meal served on the private deck outside your suite. Elsewhere, the Timeless Spa's treatments draw from the best Middle Eastern and South East Asian healing practices.

THE ST. REGIS SAADIYAT ISLAND RESORT

Saadiyat Island / *United Arab Emirates*

Saadiyat Island is a natural island of such staggering beauty; it's no surprise that Hawksbill Turtles find refuge in its pristine white sands or that the distinguished Saadiyat Beach Golf Club has found its place here. What's more, its location is ideal for guests in search of peace just 20 minutes from Abu Dhabi International Airport and minutes from downtown Abu Dhabi.

The St. Regis Saadiyat Island Resort, Abu Dhabi has received rave reviews since its launch in late 2011; proudly promoting the legendary St. Regis signature of American ingenuity and European hospitality. This luxury resort brings its own touch of Mediterranean ease and Middle Eastern colour to the experience though you'll always find the St. Regis tradition of intuitive Butler Service that caters to your every need,

from complimentary in-room drinks to packing your suitcase for your journey home.

The hotel's natural environment breathes warmth into the décor throughout the resort's living spaces that range from the intimate Superior Rooms and Suites to the majestic Royal Suite, each with its own private balcony. Unique to this location are the stunning Iridium Spa, the resort's spa; the St. Regis Athletic Club - a state-of-the-art gym; The Regal Ballroom for private events and the exclusive Sandcastle Club that takes care of entertaining guests' 1 to 12 year olds with indoor and outdoor activities.

The dazzling choice of restaurants and lounges, including 55&5th The Grill, its signature venue is world-class fare. The venues reflect the

welcoming and refined atmosphere with many of them enjoying perfect views of turquoise blue waters and the pristine white sand of Saadiyat.

PARK HYATT **JEDDAH**

Jeddah | *Saudi Arabia*

The Park Hyatt Jeddah is a versatile beach resort with a clear mission statement for business and leisure guests alike: world-class service in an unforgettable setting. Sitting in the heart of the city with the Red Sea as a backdrop, this extraordinary hotel borders the business district and is a stone's throw from the best of Jeddah's nightlife and entertainment. Noted for its striking architecture, exclusive art collection, and outstanding personalized service, the idea here is treat every guest like royalty and it shows.

There are a variety of exotic dining choices on the premises, but no matter which you choose, be sure to enjoy at least one meal on the outside terrace. This is the perfect opportunity to soak in the brilliant views of the Red Sea, sip a cocktail and sample the cuisine in style with locals and guests.

The luxury you find in the lounge and lobby extends to the guest rooms - boasting 16-foot ceilings and a neat, modern design. As with any Park Hyatt hotel, the bathrooms are also exquisite and well-appointed. In addition, the resort features a spa with separated male and female areas - that is reason enough for many guests to return to this resort.

Indeed guests stay loyal to this destination such is the feeling of peace it instills in you. You could be forgiven for thinking you were on your own private island.

KENSINGTON **PLACE**

Cape Town / *South Africa*

One of Cape Town's pioneering small boutique hotels; Kensington Place prefers to be known as a private hotel. It has an elegant designer's eye and urban escapism stamped all over it. It holds all the right elements for a flawless experience of Cape Town and all this beautiful city has to offer.

Situated on the slopes of Table Mountain, in the leafy suburb of Higgovale, the hotel is peaceful yet a stone's throw from the city centre and its hotspots. The design and ambience marry plush textures, contemporary detail with chic intimacy – there are just eight rooms, seven of them Superior Suites.

The staff is obliging and helpful and will recommend the best spots for a bite to eat or day trips and take time to make you feel special. The bar is open all hours and food is served practically all day,

excellent for a late night snack. You can relax by the pool, treat yourself with the wonderful toiletry products in your bathroom or arrange for a massage or a sports session (there's a complimentary membership to a nearby gym). The lounge area has a cosy fireplace for after-dinner relaxation and should you need to stay connected there's free Wi-Fi and a laptop at your disposal in-room and a library of films and music to enjoy. You'll sleep like a baby in your Egyptian cotton sheets ready for the next day and that sun-kissed balcony breakfast. Kensington Place is lauded by global travel experts but don't take our word for it – try it for yourself.

PEZULA PRIVATE **CASTLE**

Knysna / South Africa

How could you resist a breathtaking, private castle overlooking one of the most beautiful beaches in South Africa? Pezula Private Castle, the ultra-luxurious accommodation component of Conrad Pezula, is a spectacular escape built into the side of a cliff, with direct access to the sandy shore. Expect to live like royalty in this exclusive resort.

A stay at the Castle is as luxurious as it gets; indeed the property's philosophy is summed up as 'The luxury of being yourself'. Meals are freshly prepared in accordance with your own personal tastes and you will find the bar stocked with your favourite drinks and South African wines. You can sunbathe at the heated outdoor pool, work out in the private gym or drink cocktails in the gazebo perched above the beach.

The Castle is on an undiscovered sliver of Indian Ocean and is a magnet for high profile guests in need of rest and relaxation. The new self-contained compound consists of three buildings housing five suites in total. All three buildings are graced with soft-coloured décor enhanced with personal touches that make you feel as though you are staying in someone's home or mansion.

Guests can request a chauffeured vehicle for transfers to Conrad Pezula Resort & Spa.

Here you can enjoy further pampering at the Pezula Spa & Gym, dine in style at Zachary's restaurant or Café Z, or enjoy a great round of golf at the Pezula Championship Course.

Treat yourself to the holiday of a lifetime at Pezula Private Castle, and don't forget to bring your crown.

SINGITA **BOULDERS LODGE**

Kruger National Park | South Africa

That the Singita Boulders Lodge's wine cellar has been built around - rather than crashing through - the boulder that originally sat in the way of its construction says much about the approach this lodge takes. At every turn, the designers have made a conscious decision to work in collaboration with nature. Guests find the desert that surrounds becomes a central part of the hotel.

Inside the main resort, for example, are both lounge and dining deck areas, offering up views of the wildlife that congregates to feed at the Sand River. Those with anything more than a fleeting interest in the creatures we share our planet with are well advised to bring their camera.

Wine tastings are a popular attraction at the lodge – particularly so given the unique winery – with experienced sommeliers on hand to guide you through the premier vintages from South Africa and beyond. Selected wines here, unlikely to be found elsewhere, are available for purchase from the cellars. A great souvenir to what promises to be the holiday of a lifetime.

As if you'll need any assistance relaxing here, the Spa's complete range of treatments, which includes a fantastic deep-tissue massage, will leave you fully replenished. Leaving here you'll be ready to get back onto the wildlife trail. Alternatively a visit

to the Singita Boutique and Gallery are well worth it. Here guests can find artefacts taken from across the continent that tell some interesting stories, with many pieces created especially for Singita.

SINGITA **FARU FARU LODGE**

Grumeti Reserves / *Tanzania*

Singita Faru Faru Lodge does something very intelligent. Far from shouting from the rooftops about the sparkling suites, it quietly and seamlessly blends with the landscape, allowing the glorious country that surrounds it to do a great amount of the work.

Perched on a gentle slope, it surveys an impressive range of exotic wildlife. That the lodge draws heavily from its surroundings is clear: the infinity pool that curves along the boundary is a reflection of the watering hole lying a matter of feet below. The natural materials - stone and canvas - that work so well in combination are allied to a design that, whilst modern and comfortable, feels as if it belongs.

Similarly interactive with the remarkable African desert are the eight suites, whose open structures encourage guests to recline in their chairs and while away the day. Each has a deck where the Swarovski spotting scope comes in very handy. For a better view, head up to the elevated viewing decks, which overlook the watering hole and are a prime spot for wildlife watching.

There really is no substitute for venturing out into the wild, though, with experienced guides on hand. The best part of this is that twice daily trips are included in the suite rates. Be sure to take full advantage of both the early and late trip to

experience the way the light changes throughout the day. For those willing to pay a little extra, the balloon safari affords unparalleled views.

DIAMONDS STAR **OF THE EAST**

Zanzibar / *Tanzania*

It is hard to imagine a place spectacular enough to be named after 11 of the most precious gems in the world. The Diamond Star of the East resort on the palm tree - covered island of Zanzibar epitomizes paradise in its every form.

This resort has 11 exclusive villas with their own turquoise blue plunge pools, set against beautiful gardens with incredible views over the Indian Ocean. Just wait for the sunsets; they will literally take your breath away. Everything and anything you could dream of is catered for you at this resort - this is 24-hour butler service at its best. Don't be surprised if you find yourself begging the butlers to leave with you at the end of your holiday.

For entertainment, visit the diving centre, you are in one of the most beautiful diving spots in the world

and the marine life is worth the trip out in itself. In addition you can chance your arm at windsurfing or deep-sea fishing with special access for guests.

The Ocean Blue Restaurant gives out onto the gardens and ocean and if you end up needing a babysitter for the kids while you go to dinner, the resort will sort it out for you.

For a family-friendly holiday that loses none of its exclusivity Diamonds Star of the East has it all covered.

EXPLOREANS MARA **RIANTA CAMP**

Mara North Conservancy / Kenya

When was the last time you slept in a tent? Was it the summer before secondary school when you spent the night in a sleeping bag, cooking dinner with your friends over a campfire?

At the Mara Rianta Camp in Kenya, expect to sleep in glamorous tents quite unlike anything you have ever experienced before. These spacious tents are just a stone's throw from the edge of Africa's jungles, where wildlife roams freely.

This is the perfect base for your exclusive Safari adventures, nestled in the heart of the North Conservation Masai Mara Reserve. The camp is in the original bush with the Mara River winding around the perimeter.

Guests are awakened each morning with tea or coffee before the day begins. The sides of the

tents can be drawn up to expose the morning air, adding to the impact of sleeping in the middle of the wilderness. Don't worry though: these tents are built on elevated wooden platforms with personal viewing decks, so you can safely view the action from above.

After all of that African heat, soothe your body and mind with an invigorating massage at the Mvua African Rain Spa. The spa uses local products with healing properties for the ultimate natural experience.

Just don't be too alarmed if you wake up with a hippo outside your window in the morning. Welcome to the jungle.

TRIBE **HOTEL**
Nairobi | Kenya

When you are ready to check an African safari off your bucket list, we recommend Tribe Hotel. Here is a setting in which sophisticated elegance juxtaposes the rustic plains of Nairobi, Kenya to stunning effect. There's a sense that the hotel has consciously taken hospitality back to its nomadic roots; to a time when weary travelers were greeted with warmth and taken into the comforts of a private home. Now, this 'home' is a lavish resort where a genuine welcome and impeccable service are par for the course.

Tribe is nothing short of breathtaking. The modern loft style rooms and sleek architecture are reminiscent of the streets of Manhattan. The African art on display throughout the hotel however will give you a sense of the local culture peppered with warm colours and wood interspersed with steel and glass - the overall effect is highly distinctive.

When you walk through the main entrance, you come into a lively lobby dotted with stylish and artistic furniture, where guests can lounge and chat to the sounds of funky tunes. This is the perfect place for a few afternoon cocktails.

The spacious, modern suites are adorned with African statues and luxuriously large beds.

There is also a library containing some 2,800 books and 300 DVDs for those rainy days when you just can't pull yourself out of bed alongside the 24-hour room service rustles up the finest international and local cuisine.

At Tribe, the staff goes out of its way to make sure you have the perfect African experience without compromising on luxury - there is even a limousine service to and from the airport and guest security is a priority. Village Market, East Africa's largest shopping and recreation complex with over 150 shops and boutiques is a perfect spot to visit for picking up interesting souvenirs and hand-crafted art work.

A day out on safari is one of the most exhilarating experiences you can have in the wild short of bungee jumping (or white-water rafting!) but it can be a long day so an effective way to reflect on your day is to unwind at the award-winning Kaya spa. Treatments leave you feeling refreshed and relaxed, conjuring the wonders of the Kenyan forests without leaving the comfort of the modern, chic studio. What's more, Tribe's most striking design feature is the outdoor pool with its priceless views. Friends can dine on 'floating' islands just beyond the main restaurant and couples lounge by a fireplace set inside the swimming pool. You can take advantage of the African sunshine and sunbathe in the tropical setting of waterfalls and beautiful gardens.

Gourmets are in for a treat with the culinary delights of Jiko that prizes fresh ingredients and the very best imports. Although they have a mouth-watering menu, the kitchen can accommodate any additional requests.

In the meantime you might see a lion or two.

MZIMA **HOUSE**

Galu Beach / *Kenya*

Tucked away on the white beaches of the Indian Ocean, lies a tropical oasis just waiting to be discovered. The recently built Mzima is a grand beach house on Kenya's beautiful Diani Beach where guests come to escape reality and which - trust us - it is difficult to leave.

The villa is arranged around a large swimming pool, cushioned by lush tropical gardens that stand between the house and the ocean; providing plenty of room to lounge and enjoy freshly-made juice and hors d'oeuvres.

Tunisian and Roman influences run through the house with rich details and warm colours while Mzima features five en-suite bedrooms for up to 10 guests. The views are out of this world looking out onto a palm tree-lined horizon and yielding some legendary sunsets.

For those in need of pampering, the house offers a therapeutic spa room where you can have a manicure or a restorative back massage from professionals using local oils and techniques. No need to worry about dining options in this remote location - Mzima House is a unique experience with an exceptional Swahili chef on hand to dish up your private meals.

Guests can enjoy dhow safaris, cultural village tours, snorkeling and even take micro-light flights over Diani beach.

There is something very special about taking your comfort and luxury to new lengths (and heights) and it comes highly recommended at Mzima House.

FRÉGATE **ISLAND PRIVATE**

Frégate Island | Seychelles

They say great things come in small packages. Frégate Island Private is a perfect example of this; capturing all that is good about a tropical retreat in the space of just under two square miles. With its abundance of lush vegetation and seven pristine white sand beaches, one of these voted among the most beautiful the world over, the resort is a veritable picture postcard of a holiday destination. The preservation of the natural environment is taken very seriously, meaning that guests get to enjoy an unusually vast array of flora and fauna, including 2,000 Giant Aldabra Tortoises and 101 rare bird species.

There are just 16 spacious one or two bedroom villas here – exclusivity being a top priority. Friendly private butler service provides 24-hour assistance to make your stay truly memorable and each villa has a large, private infinity pool, Jacuzzi and a spacious outdoor terrace.

A lovely additional touch is the island's very own plantation that uses hydroponics. Here you'll be treated to fresh, organic fruit and vegetables produced on the island every day, which are so good they are also used in the Rock Spa treatments too!

Dine at Frégate House or try out the offerings from Plantation House, where traditional Creole specialties are served either al fresco or inside the building that operates by day as a museum. The motto being "anything, anywhere, anytime", guests are encouraged to enjoy their meal at their favourite spot- be that on the beach, in the Tree House, the Marina & Yacht Club or in the comfort of their own villa.

MARADIVA

Flic en Flac / *Mauritius*

If you're searching for the holiday of a lifetime, that combines romance, intimacy and authentic character, Maradiva Villas Resort & Spa has it all in spades. A haven of luxury set in 27 acres of tropical landscape on the west coast of Mauritius; Maradiva prides itself on friendly, discreet staff and a sense of privacy and exclusivity. Each of the 65 guest villas has its own plunge pool and terrace with adjoining dining and living space as well as stunning views of the ocean or of the lush surrounding gardens.

Food lovers are in for a treat at the Pan Asian Cilantro restaurant - complete with a fabulous Teppanyaki Counter - and the Coast2Coast restaurant. Both offer diverse international cuisine with regularly updated menus that showcase the freshest and finest produce, mostly sourced directly from the Chef's garden, while

the Breakers Bar is a perfect spot for whiling away the hours in a relaxed environment.

The facilities include water sports, a fitness centre and kids club, but the jewel in Maradiva's crown is the Maradiva Spa. Be sure to set a day aside for this award-winning holistic spa that sets new standards in the art of Ayurvedic treatments. Qualified therapists guide you through the traditional Indian treatments and ancient healing therapies to ensure you come away feeling totally rejuvenated.

We guarantee you'll be planning your next stay here by the time you've checked into your villa on the first day...

THE ST. REGIS MAURITIUS RESORT

Le Morne | Mauritius

Situated in the Indian Ocean, east of Madagascar, the island of Mauritius is an unspoilt tropical paradise just waiting to be discovered. Offering sun, sea and sand it encapsulates the classic getaway holiday.

However, as we discovered, there isn't much conformity to be found wherever you look. From the moment you step inside and are treated to the signature St. Regis personal butler service, are gifted your monogrammed stationery and seen to your room, the whole experience just seems so reassuringly tailored. Nowhere is this clearer than at the Iridium Spa, where treatments are honed to suit individual tastes and needs.

Epicureans will similarly relish the offerings of renowned Executive Head Chef Olivier Belliard who oversees the design of menus in all six of the resort's restaurants. The sheer abundance of choice begs the question-where to go? Our pick of an admittedly stellar bunch is 'Inspiration'. Identified as Mauritius' smallest, and probably most exclusive restaurant, its seating arrangement allows diners the chance to see into the kitchen and experience the finest food at a three-star Michelin level. Here comes the truly great part – he openly discusses the inspiration behind each of the dishes cooked up before your eyes.

Taking time to explore further afield, kite surfing at Le Morne must be high on the list for the more adventurous traveller. The host of the annual kite surfing world cup, it is the sport's top global destination. Its status as a UNESCO World Heritage Site makes this fact easy to understand.

SHANGRI-LA'S VILLINGILI **RESORT & SPA**

Villingili Island | *Maldives*

Shangri-La's Villingili Resort and Spa, Maldives is the first luxury destination south of the equator on the island of Villingili at the southern-most tip of the Addu Atoll. Picture a scene where vegetation is so lush and plentiful, lagoons and nature trails so untouched, you'd be forgiven for thinking this beauty was man-made. And that's where you'd be wrong. The resort enjoys kilometres of sandy beach and has organically blended the seven distinct styles of villa accommodation into their natural environment. Private Ocean Villas and Tree-House Retreats feel spacious and stylish with decked terraces, outdoor showers, freestanding bath tubs, private pools and the ocean on your doorstep.

Your villa host will fix you a cocktail, book you a treatment at the fabulous CHI, The Spa or invite you for a spectacular round of golf in what is the Maldives' first and only course. For extra glamour, why not hire a luxury yacht and have your lunch on the equator?

PARK HYATT **MALDIVES HADAHAA**

North Huvadhoo (Gaafu Alifu) Atoll | *Maldives*

Hyatt's first luxury hotel in the Maldives, Park Hyatt Maldives Hadahaa is a hidden paradise. Situated on an equatorial island in the North Huvadhoo (Gaafu Alifu) Atoll, the hotel is set against a backdrop of the Indian Ocean's pristine, coral-filled waters. Located 400km south of Malé and only 56 km from the Equator, the hotel's remote location means that it's only accessible via private transfer by speedboat. This isn't just another secluded hotel; it's the ultimate hideaway. As soon as you step off the boat onto the immaculate white sand, you're guaranteed complete tranquillity a million miles away from the intrusions of the outside world.

From the rooms to the restaurants, the spa to the service, every aspect of this restful resort is aimed at helping you unwind. The accommodation is made up of just 50 villas set either amidst the lush vegetation of the island or on stilts over the sea. Each of these suspended Park Water Villas offers panoramic 180° views as well as direct access to the crystalline Indian Ocean. Step inside your villa and you'll find all the modern technology as well as the services of a dedicated Personal Host at your beck and call.

Days here are spent swimming in the pool overlooking the ocean, taking a private yoga class or trying one of the signature treatments at the Vidhun Spa. Nestled amongst the lush native flora of the island, the spa hosts five private couples treatment villas for the ultimate in private pampering. For dinner, choose between the international gourmet menu at The Dining Room or regionally inspired dishes at the Island

Grill. The Island Grill's food is the gastronomic incarnation of that indulgent holiday feeling. As you walk back to your villa, don't forget to look up. The hotel lies just 56 kilometres from the equator, affording it a unique view of constellations from both the northern and southern hemispheres. Devoid of artificial light sources, the night sky is crystal clear and perfect for star-gazing.

But here it's the diving which reigns supreme. The hotel boasts its own house coral reef which, encircling the island, sits just 30 metres from the beach. Rich with a diverse marine wildlife, the Hadahaa House Reef claims the largest coral coverage of all 1900 islands of the Maldives, complete with 250 species of coral and 1200 species of fish. With the hotel's five-star PADI Dive and Activity Centre, you can choose to snorkel amongst the fish or dive to new depths with a private scuba diving lesson. The waters here are truly unbeatable, filled with undiscovered natural treasures just waiting to be explored.

Of course, the hotel is hopelessly romantic too, offering breathtakingly beautiful exotic weddings. But it isn't just another hotel geared towards honeymooners – Park Hyatt Maldives Hadahaa provides any discerning traveller with the perfect relaxing vacation.

For the most luxurious way to appreciate the island's starry skies, head to the beach. Perched on the sand are the hotel's beach cabanas – perfect for star-gazing with a glass of premier cru champagne.

JUMEIRAH **VITTAVELI**
Bolifushi Island / *Maldives*

It's hard to imagine that Male International Airport is only 20 minutes from the utterly tranquil Jumeirah Vittaveli on Bolifushi Island.

The luxurious air-conditioned timber villas are graced with high ceilings and state of the art amenities (Apple Media Centre, flat screen TV and IPod dock), to feel like a five-star residence. The open-space layout affords stunning sea views wherever you are and every villa boasts a private pool. Additionally, take time to enjoy the extensive maxi bar. The resort enjoys four dining venues - namely Samsara with its Asian and Maldivian specialities and Fenesse that sits dreamily overlooking the lagoon waters.

Apart from treatments at the world-class Talise Spa, you can try your hand at yoga or take part in water sports activities. There's also a fitness centre and extensive Kids Club facilities, complete with an arts & crafts centre, family pool and a recreation centre for teenagers. A little way along the beach is the Mu Beach Bar and Grill, a friendly restaurant which also plays host every evening to a fish feeding, where large numbers of exotic fish congregate to great effect.

BAROS MALDIVES **RESORT & SPA**

North Male' Atoll / Maldives

The Maldives are synonymous with honeymooning couples and idyllic tropical islands. Baros Maldives is no exception. Oozing romance and privacy, this small resort is perfect if you want to escape the stresses of everyday life. You can expect total peace and tranquillity - there are no noisy water sports and no children under eight. Now how appealing does that sound?

If that's not enough to tempt you then the personalised service will win you over. Every aspect of your holiday is focused around making your stay special to you: from a chat with the Executive Chef over your food preferences to bespoke dive programmes. Even at the spa, the team will devise a series of treatments (from the plethora of options) especially to suit your needs and guaranteed to leave you feeling pampered and relaxed.

The piece de resistance has to be the house reef that's just a few metres' swim from the beach (easily accessible even for timid snorkellers) and bursting with marine life, and if you're an experienced diver there are enough nearby dive sites to explore to keep you happy for at least a week! If you'd prefer not to venture underwater, you won't be missing out - simply pick a spot on your overwater terrace and watch turtles and rays glide past, or visit the Marine Centre and adopt your own coral and you'll receive an updated picture every six months (a truly unique holiday memory!)

And we haven't even mentioned the mouth-watering food (don't leave without enjoying a romantic sandbank dinner) and secluded Pool Villas.

COCO **BODU HITHI**
North Malé Atoll | *Maldives*

A visit to the Coco Bodu Hithi resort is almost as much about the journey as it is the stay. The stunning private island skirted by pristine white sandy beaches - which hosts the resort's 100 villas - lies a 40-minute speedboat journey from Male. It is with good reason that Coco Bodu Hithi is put forward as the ultimate tropical island hideaway.

The unforgettable journey that bookends your stay sets the tone for much of what is to come, with each and every villa oozing Maldivian charm. The 44 Island Villas, for example, provide direct access to the beach from their setting within lush vegetation. The 32 Water Villas and Escape Water Villas perched high on wooden stilts above the turquoise ocean lead to the lagoon, where guests can swim or snorkel at their leisure. Most impressive are the Escape Water Residences where withdrawal is top of the menu – set far from the mainland, escape is absolute. The private deck and pavilion provide the perfect vantage point from which to enjoy sunsets that border on perfection.

Villas throughout the resort are luxurious, with oversized bathtubs the centrepiece of lavish bathrooms. King-sized beds furnish spacious rooms, and all villas open out onto terraces accompanied by private pools. The outdoor space available at each villa really is priceless when surroundings are as stunning as these.

Dining options are impressively diverse, ranging all the way from Asian fusion through to local Maldivian cuisine. A particular highlight is Aqua, where guests sample the finest freshly caught seafood while sitting atop decking raised over lapping water. Dishes here are distinctly Asian, featuring subtly spiced variations that are perfectly complemented by the extensive wine menu.

There seems little chance of a stressful day spent here, though for those in pursuit of absolute relaxation, Coco Spa has a full range of treatments on offer. Each is administered in an environment conducive to unwinding. Looking out across the Indian Ocean while enjoying a massage and reflecting on the holiday of your dreams is surely a 'pinch yourself' moment if ever there was one!

At the other end of the spectrum adventurers are similarly well-catered for, with kayaking, snorkelling and sailing all on offer. Deep-sea fishing, scuba diving and reef planting excursions allow for a full appreciation of the vibrant array of marine life that calls the Maldives home.

BANYAN TREE **MADIVARU**

Madivaru Island • Maldives

Accessible by seaplane or private sailboat, Banyan Tree Madivaru is the ideal island-destination for escaping reality. With only six tented villas and each with its own private pool and direct access to the beach, this island paradise promises guests absolute seclusion and exclusivity.

Time literally stands still at this tropical sanctuary, where there are no deadlines and no times to adhere to. Instead, each guest is encouraged to relax, swim and most importantly dine anywhere, any time (arranged by their villa host), be it a private Champagne breakfast on a sandbank or a three-course dinner in their villa. A pair of spa beds can be set up for private in-villa treatments from the world famous Banyan Tree Spa, or guests can explore the pleasures of the Indian Ocean by snorkelling or taking dolphin safaris. Banyan Tree Madivaru guarantees every guest a unique and unforgettable Robinson Crusoe experience.

JUMEIRAH **DHEVANAFUSHI**
Gaafu Alifu Atoll / Maldives

Jumeirah Dhevanafushi is the ultimate honeymoon destination but will suit anyone trying to get away from it all.

Lying untouched in the Southern Maldives, what is really striking upon arrival is the purity of the surroundings. Eight Island Revives and a unique Island Sanctuary lie nestled in lush vegetation that is interspersed with scented walkways, while the thirteen beachside Revive suites stand suspended over the Indian Ocean. All the suites are spacious and boast their own swimming pool and 24-hour butler service. Try the signature spa and bath rituals in the privacy of your own suite, as well as at the world-class Talise Spa, which stands over the water and gives spectacular views.

The food is out of this world with three restaurants: Johara, Mumayaz and Azara and an equally memorable

experience is the off-island picnic organised through the resort team. The spectacular coral reef is perfect for snorkeling and diving. Take a 15-minute speedboat ride and enjoy a picnic lunch with champagne in the middle of the ocean.

ADITYA **BOUTIQUE HOTEL**
Galle / Sri Lanka

Aditya Boutique Hotel in Sri Lanka has made it a mission to wow its guests by delivering a life-changing experience and it works. We are in an exclusive 12-suite boutique resort on a secluded stretch of beach in Rathgama where the order of day is discretion and unbridled luxury. Each suite is a self-contained 'apartment' with spacious sleeping, living and bathroom areas topped off by a stunning outdoor plunge pool and balcony with garden or ocean views. Be sure to choose from the pillow menu for an even greater night's sleep!

Menus are available 24 hours a day with a firm emphasis on locally-sourced seafood. Particularly enticing is the promise of any meal available at any time, in any place. The hotel has its own pool with waiter service and there's a widely extensive collection of books in the library alongside movies and music. The Nirvana spa, a gym and an on-site yoga instructor on request, complete the feel-good factor. Should you wish to venture out we recommend the whale-watching expeditions and bike rides to explore the area's most interesting spots.

107

THE FORTRESS **RESORT & SPA**

Galle / *Sri Lanka*

The Fortress is well aware of its historical roots. The resort's design centres around the influence of Dutch and Portuguese colonisers, as well as drawing heavily from Sri Lankan history and the effect is stunning. Add these unique features to the coastal location that affords barely believable views out onto the Indian Ocean and you have the recipe for an unforgettable escape.

Much of this interest in the area's charming culture can also be found in the resort's 53 rooms. Stylishly accessorized, the modern Sri Lankan decor fuses beautifully with soothing soft, dark tones. Luxurious furnishings, like Egyptian Frette linen and king-sized beds, and the latest in technology keep guests fully entertained in comfort. However, the abundance of attractions outside makes it difficult to spend much time inside.

Among these is the Spa Naturel, where guests can indulge in a day's relaxation. A complimentary bath of flower petals is available as a great precursor to the luxurious massage - a must for stress busting.

The sheer variety of menu choices from the resort's three restaurants means you certainly won't be left disappointed. Discover the wonders of fine Sri Lankan cuisine at Pepper, where horizon views serve as a priceless backdrop, or venture to Heat for international dishes. Best of all, enjoy a meal in a spot of your choosing – on the star-lit beach for example!

ANANDA IN THE **HIMALAYAS**

Rishikesh / India

India is the birthplace of the ancient arts of yoga, meditation and Ayurveda making the Ananda in the Himalayas spa a great starting point for a holistic life. Flawless staff and service have rightfully earned this luxury spa its multiple industry awards. Where else can you kick start the day with a yoga session that boasts the Himalayas as a backdrop? It's hard to believe you're only 45 minutes by air from New Delhi. Ananda is renowned for its spa's signature wellness programs, like the detox, weight loss and ayurvedic rejuvenation. These are tailored to the individual so be sure to book a session. The serene surroundings overlooking the Rishikesh Valley make even the most arduous hill trek seem enjoyable! The exquisite meals contain the finest organic produce, after which you can retreat to your room where your evening bath has been run. In this tranquil environment the focus is you

and the team ensures you escape the stresses of daily life. Something you surely deserve...

CONTENTS ASIA AND PACIFIC

I've had a number of experiences in Asia over the years. These have ranged from the carefree and unplanned, to the intense and profound (with a pinch of glamour along the way). I have memories of throwing on a large backpack as a youngster; excited at the prospect of an island-hopping adventure in Thailand. I've done my fair share of sun bathing on a surf board and sipping exotic cocktails from coconuts in Bali; I've explored the bustling streets of Kowloon as a graduate, immersing myself in the Mandarin language. I assumed that when it came to Asia I had a good, strong idea of what it was all about, of how I would feel.

Tokyo had never been on my radar; I think I always assumed it was too far away for a holiday and that it was somewhere only business men visited to continue their corporate chase - the concept of learning Japanese was not even a consideration. More fool me. So when the opportunity arose to spend five days in Tokyo, I accepted without truly realising what a city of mind-boggling contrasts I was about to discover.

I had always thought - somewhat cynically - that 'love at first sight' was a cliché best reserved for classic novels, poems or, at best, a cracking pop song; until Palace Hotel Tokyo that is. As I stood there before this extraordinary building, gazing at its impressive façade, I knew I had fallen hook, line and sinker. Palace Hotel Tokyo stands tall on the edge of the Imperial Palace gardens, as any palace would. Its curved exterior feels like a visual embrace; welcoming you to the city and its people, safeguarding its heritage. I was mesmerised and couldn't wait to get inside and discover what lay beyond these walls.

Accompanied by my porter as we moved towards the oak door, I was struck by the beauty of the art piece on display (which I later learned was that of the Japanese artist Okamura). The yellow elephant, famous for being carved in wood

stared out proudly nodding, as if to greet me – appealing to my long-lost sense of romance. As I remained staring at the friendly elephant, I could feel someone sidle up alongside me. "Isn't he marvellous?" a deep voice resounded, "Have you seen the rabbit? He is a powerful creature, found in one of the 20th floor suites. If you like this piece, you will love Mr. Rabbit" I turned to respond but he'd gone, leaving nothing but a faint whiff of whisky in the air. I turned to my porter with his knowing smile and he duly led me to my suite.

My suite was extraordinary and overlooked a spectacular Tokyo sky line; a vast and swirling canvas of bleeding orange, pink and white that announced an impending sunset. Looking down, the stillness of the Imperial Palace and its moat-side were strangely reassuring. I turned to admire the room and my crisp white bed, so inviting in the middle of it (that jetlag is a killer). When I turned back to the balcony, the view had already changed

with the onset of night fall. Tokyo's electric skyline lay before me, in all its frantically twinkling glory. My thoughts turned to aperitifs and tuna tartare.

After freshening up in my ultra-sleek bathroom, I slipped on my finery and headed down from the dizzying heights of the 21st floor to the impossibly chic Lounge Bar Privé on the 6th. Perched at the bar, sipping champagne, is the perfect spot for taking in the views across the city. Guests famously come to relax in and enjoy the peace and quiet of this sophisticated spot and enjoy a mean signature Gin Fizz or smoky martini. Through the floor-to-ceiling glass walls I caught the reflection of a gentleman stirring his drink. Our eyes locked and he smiled. As he walked over to me I recognised the faint whiff of whisky. "So did you venture to the 20th floor?'" I shake my head. "No, I have been admiring the palace and sky views for too long. However, I could sit and ponder on this bar's incredible décor for just as long".

The gentleman explained that the lush, green palace gardens had been purposely recreated in the bar's interior design. An impressive leaf-shaped bar fronts some intricate branch-like metal work behind the selection of vintage alcoholic drinks. The carpet resembles a forest canopy floor on a summer's day; all sun-dappled light and soft shadows. My new friend said, "It is impressive isn't it? If you're an art enthusiast please let me show you the hotel's collection. It's very special." With that we wandered down to Grand Kitchen, the hotel's al fresco restaurant, where a moat-side table was laid out on the terrace. I sat down, hugging a large, comfy cushion and admired the swans gently floating by. There was something disarmingly relaxed about this restaurant; an unexpected home from home in a vibrant albeit daunting city. Photos of the kitchen staff graced the walls while they worked their magic in the open-plan kitchen in full view of diners. Grand Kitchen reminded

As my time at the Palace continued I found myself increasingly struck by the art pieces dotted around the hotel. The gentleman I met on my first night was absolutely right; Okamura's rabbit is amazing, as is his sophisticated dragon in Royal Bar. His pieces are all of animals or creatures depicted in Japanese myths and made from cedar wood.

As I continued my own personal art tour, I found myself staring at an oversized floral piece on the second floor. By artist Satoshi Uchiumi, this oil on canvas called 'Under the Colours' immediately attracts your attention. However, possibly my favourite work in the hotel was the chalk tableau piece located in Grand Kitchen. Entitled 'A Brand New Yesterday' it celebrates Palace Hotel Tokyo's 51-year history. Another piece of art that really caught my attention was the individually framed trio of embossed prints on paper placed in the lifts. I later learned these were created by Scottish artist Jenny Smith, known in her native land for cutting-edge laser work. I found her artwork to be contemporary, visually enchanting and a wonderful representation of British art.

On my final night spent at Palace Hotel Tokyo, I visited its teppanyaki restaurant. Salmon and potato cakes, shrimp with a light cheese crisp and the premium Japanese beef flavoured with the subtle tang of natural salt – everything was prepared to absolute perfection and accompanied by a precise choice of wine, courtesy of the excellent sommelier. Finishing with a cold glass of sake I headed to Lounge Bar Privé for one last night cap.

Apart from the astounding beauty of the hotel and its faultless staff and service, the magical touches are what made my experience here so unforgettable. Little bedside cups of ice to pop into my water, delightful patisserie and marshmallows to keep me going and personal attention to detail left me feeling like the most important guest ever to grace Palace Hotel Tokyo.

me of my kitchen at home and watching my mother prepare dinner. I was in safe hands.

After a wonderfully restful night's sleep, I woke to the sounds of well, nothing. This was my time to enjoy the delights of my bathroom and my shower. When I stepped back into the room there was a tray of fresh fruit, Japanese green tea and natural yogurt waiting for me. Nestled in-between my plate and bowl I found a small book with 'evian SPA TOKYO' embossed on the front. I decided it was a perfect day for indulging in a treatment and after seconds of contemplation I opted for a 'Revitalising Jet-Lag Therapy' which claimed to fight fatigue and stimulate the senses and I swiftly ventured down to the 5th floor. The spa is inspired by the evian ethos of purity, with a fusion of French teaching and Asian massage. I was greeted by a gentle lady who took me to the pre-treatment room where I was invited to

lie down, sip green tea and nibble on an apricot. Ten minutes later I was led to a low-lit room and so started my treatment. With emphasis on releasing tension on my upper back and neck, my therapist instinctively knew what I needed and dripped warm aromatherapy oil over my head before embarking on a re-mineralizing and restorative journey. When I finally came round to a soothing hand massage I realised it was the first time that I had felt truly rested for some time. Soon after my final glass of camomile tea I floated away on a cloud to enjoy my afternoon tea.

The Palace Afternoon Tea is certainly one of a kind compared to other leading hotels. An impressive selection of Japanese and Chinese tea was served while I chose from the Jyubako (a tiered lacquer ware box) filled with various snacks, of which the Quiche Lorraine and petit gâteau were particular highlights.

AMANKORA

Bhutan

Amankora has quite literally opened the door to visitors seeking an ultra- luxurious experience of Bhutan with a series of lodges scattered through this Himalayan kingdom's central and western valleys.

Amankora Paro is the 24-suite flagship while Amankora Punakha is an eight-suite retreat set in an orange orchard overlooking the rice fields. The 16-suite Amankora Thimphu is in the Thimphu Valley, Amankora Gangtey is another eight-suite remote valley retreat and Amankora Bumthang offers 16 suites next to one of Bhutan's royal palaces and all of these spectacular sites are easily accessible from each other.

The landscape is out of this world and there's enough cultural wealth to feed the mind and soul of any kind of traveller. Aman make it a mission to pamper guests so take advantage of the excellent services on offer- take a guided tour and book that spa treatment in the knowledge that you'll be living in the finest luxury that Bhutan has to offer.

UMA **BY COMO**

Bhutan

Located in Bhutan — a remote Himalayan and entirely Buddhist kingdom — are the Uma Paro and Uma Punakha resorts. Both of these offer unbridled escape filled with cultural discovery and physical adventure in two important valleys a five-hour drive apart.

The Punakha Valley is one of the most precious in the eyes of the Bhutanese and within it are two historic sites that are unmissable when visiting Uma Punakha — the Temple of the Divine Madam and the Punakha Dzong.

There are two types of accommodation at Punakha— the Valley Room or a Villa. Whichever choice you make, you'll be relaxing in style. Forest view and valley view rooms make the most of the location, overlooking verdant valley slopes and the Mo Chu River. Vistas from the larger villas, designed by traditionally-schooled Bhutanese artists, are similarly breathtaking.

The mission statement of the Uma resorts is clear: to immerse travellers in the local culture. This is why the resort works hard, along with its sister property, Uma Paro to create perfectly tailored itineraries, from hiking to biking to whitewater rafting.

Like Panakha, Uma Paro offers you many opportunities to do as little or as much as you would like. Bukhari, Uma Paro's flagship restaurant, features cuisine that sources ingredients locally, making fine alterations to dishes that have been refined from generation to generation. There are also daily yoga classes, meditation areas, a hot-stone bathhouse, and an indoor pool.

CHINA **WORLD SUMMIT WING**

Beijing / *China*

The crystal chandelier in the lift is a suitably dazzling indication of what lies in store at the China World Summit Wing. Stepping out onto the 64th floor is a spectacular experience. The Residents' Foyer with its stylish sofas is the perfect setting for a spot of spying. The handy telescopes are a lovely touch and as you survey the expansive skyline it's hard not to feel like you're on top of the world. That's because by China's standards you are. The CWSW is the tallest building and hotel in Beijing. At 330 metres above the China World Trade Center it sits in

the heart of the Central Business District and is visible from many locations within the city.

The 278 guest rooms are the largest hotel rooms to be found in all of Beijing. All have dramatic floor-to-ceiling windows offering unlimited views over the ever-changing cityscape. The rooms are classically decorated with subtle Chinese touches and there are luxurious amenities such as fluffy goose-down duvets and pillows, infinity-style bathtubs, stocks of L'Occitane toiletries, and convenient electric blackout blinds.

If you're seeking refuge from the sights and sounds of the big city, the CWSW is also a lifestyle sanctuary. CHI, The Spa at Shangri-La caters to all of your pampering needs with a choice of 25 different treatments. The Amber Facial and Jade Stone Massage are unforgettable and both unique to the hotel; designed to reenergize and balance your body and soul. Located on the 78th floor, the health club caters to all levels of fitness, with a wide selection of gym machines looking out on the city, an infinity pool with underwater music, and sauna and steam rooms.

When the beautifying and exercising are done with, guests have five restaurants and bars to choose from, all offering a suitably varied selection of menus and cocktails. Grill 79, the hotel's signature modern steakhouse, is the highest restaurant in town and features an international menu categorized by raw, vegetarian, from the ocean and from the grill. The other restaurants specialize in gourmet Chinese, Japanese, and European cuisine. However, the Atmosphere Bar steals the show. As the highest bar in town, it boasts a ceiling depicting a constellation of delicate stars, and in the evenings live music that attracts a cool cocktail crowd and an elegantly relaxed atmosphere.

For those looking to host a meeting or private event, the hotel has elegant private dining rooms and ballrooms, most with natural light. Designed for both small and large events, these include the fully equipped 95-seat auditorium and rooftop garden space. The hotel staff will see that all the arrangements go smoothly so guests don't have to worry about anything.

In the end, guests never need come down from the remarkable heights of the CWSW, and truthfully, we wouldn't blame you.

ST. REGIS **BEIJING**

Beijing / China

A regal establishment located in the heart of Beijing's diplomatic, business, and shopping centres, the St. Regis Beijing is the perfect place for the most distinguished world traveller. This well-known gem is a gathering spot for government officials, foreign dignitaries, journalists and business executives of the highest calibre.

The room choices are impressive with 258 elegantly appointed guestrooms and suites designed with subtle modern Asian touches. Highly recommended for an unforgettable stay is the Presidential Suite. With a dining room that can comfortably seat up to ten and a large kitchen, this space is meant for entertaining or holding meetings and interviews as if guests were in their private homes. A great place to escape from the bustle of the city is the fitness

centre which offers everything from aroma steam rooms to a driving and putting golf range. You can even plunge into the natural hot springs that rise naturally from below the St. Regis Spa.

Gourmet diners have some mouth-watering options that include fine Western and traditional Asian cuisine. Be sure to try Danieli's, "Beijing's Finest Italian Restaurant," for rustic yet elegant Italian specialities, not to mention the city's largest wine list. For an extensive selection of world-class cigars, check out the Cigar Lounge in the Press Club Bar, where you can also sample a staggering 50 plus cocktails.

Be it business or pleasure, St. Regis Beijing brings that extra touch of magic to China's ancient capital.

FUCHUN **RESORT**

Fuyang / *China*

Fuchun Resort takes full advantage of its unique setting, embedded as it is within the fertile lands of Fuyang, China. Just two and a half hours from Shanghai, the hotel is situated in 150 acres of land that holds a working tea plantation.

Designed with the region's rich cultural heritage in mind – the landscape was immortalised in a famous 14th-century painting – the resort aims to capture the spirit of a traditional Chinese village during the Southern Song Dynasty. Consequently, water, wood and stone feature heavily throughout. We advise experimenting with some traditional Hangzhou cuisine at the Asian Corner restaurant. The lanterns, screens and daybeds recreate an authentic Chinese atmosphere.

The award-winning Fuchun Spa informed by local healing traditions is a very pleasant distraction,

as is the 18-hole professional golf course that weaves its way through the tea plantation. The Lake Lounge offers a complimentary night-cap after 9pm, and the best views are found here.

THE **PENINSULA**

Hong Kong | China

The Peninsula Hong Kong first opened its doors in 1928 and has since been regarded as one of the most elegant, sophisticated hotels in the world. It deserves this accolade thanks to its sumptuous décor and exceptional service. Staff go out of their way for you and are nothing short of professional. The hotel's stunningly remodeled rooms and suites exhibit the finest materials and craftsmanship and boast a bespoke residential feel seamlessly blended with leading-edge technology. You're surrounded by panoramic views - be it from the picture postcard windows in your suite, The Peninsula Spa or the swimming pool and sun terrace. The hotel commands spectacular views of Victoria Harbour and Hong Kong Island. There's also an unrivalled choice of top-notch restaurants to choose from and The Peninsula Afternoon Tea at The Lobby- a veritable institution- makes this hotel a 'must' on your wish list of the world's finest establishments.

ISLAND **SHANGRI-LA**

Hong Kong / *China*

From the moment you walk through the doors to the moment you check out, your time and presence are considered precious at Island Shangri-La in Hong Kong. You'll be greeted by exceptionally friendly guest relations staff that quickly catch onto your personal tastes and greet you by name. As you mop your brow with the hot towel and sip Chinese tea served in-room, you quickly realise you're in excellent hands. You'll also notice a deliciously serene scent as you move around the public areas – it was created especially for the hotel - suffused with delicate notes of ginger, bergamot, woods and vanilla.

From the impressive entrance, guests can take the lift to level 39 and change to the bubble lift to view the world's largest Chinese silk painting, the Great Motherland of China, hanging 51 metres into an atrium. There are more than 771 chandeliers throughout the hotel, including one in every guest room. All the rooms and suites are extremely spacious, fitted with beautiful Chinese antique furnishings and boast incredible views of the city and Victoria Harbour or Victoria Peak. There are lovely touches everywhere - L'Occitane toiletries in the guestrooms and Bvlgari in the suites. Every bathroom is fitted with a television and the beds and pillows are superbly crisp and plump -the linen comes courtesy of Frette- and you'll sleep like a baby. The breakfast buffet at cafe TOO is largely recognized as being the best anywhere in the world with its top quality service and the freshest foods that cover a great range of world cuisines including Japanese and traditional Chinese.

The Lobby lounge is great to sit in even as a solo traveller. Every day between 3 and 7pm a music quartet entertains guests and you can have a bite to eat while you watch them perform. Choose any national newspaper to catch up on world events or make the most of the free Wi-Fi available throughout the entire hotel, in the hotel's fleet of limousines for those lucky enough to enjoy the chauffeur service, as well in the rooftop Horizon Club. This state-of-the-art exclusive lounge is ideal for business travellers seeking peace as they contemplate the Hong Kong skyline and there's a 24-hour health club to keep up the fitness regime. As you order round-the-clock room service you can't help thinking that mysterious perfumer managed to capture the very soul of this hotel as its scent and memories linger on.

PARESA

Phuket / *Thailand*

You'll be forgiven for thinking you've landed in heaven as you arrive at Paresa Resort in Phuket. In fact, the word "Paresa" translates to "heaven of all heavens" and the name is certainly no exaggeration! An accommodating team of "angels" (Paresa's concierge staff) go out of their way to ensure your stay is as blissful as possible; from a fresh bowl of fruit waiting for you upon arrival, to a selection of tasty canapes brought to your room every evening.

Sitting atop the cliffs of Kamala, Paresa blends harmoniously with its tropical surroundings. It's built around magnificent Banyan trees that provide natural shade for the al fresco restaurant and glorious infinity pool. Sitting under their leafy canopies you can really absorb the tranquillity of this paradise place. Each of Paresa's open-plan villas overlooks the Andaman Sea, and if you're lucky

enough to stay in the top floor Cielo Residence you'll experience truly breathtaking views. Huge bath tubs, luxury bed linen and private plunge pools complete this picture of utter luxury.

Paresa's cookery school hosts daily classes, where you can learn how to make classic Thai dishes with fresh ingredients bought from the local market. But if your culinary skills aren't up to scratch, Paresa's amazing restaurants (Italian or Thai) will provide so many options to satisfy your gastronomic needs. For a romantic experience you'll never forget, dine on a 'private island' in the beautifully lit infinity pool. You'll feel like you're floating in a star-lit sky.

THE RACHA **AND ANUMBA SPA**

Phuket / Thailand

As you depart from Phuket aboard the Racha's private, luxury speedboat, the daily stresses palpably fade away. Half an hour later, as you round upon the tiny, jewel-like island of Racha Yai, you'll have forgotten that a blackberry would be anything other than a fruit for this is a haven of tranquility. Don't be embarrassed if you catch your breath as you first glimpse a view of the island; the captain is used to it and this place is nothing less than postcard-picture-perfect.

The resort is set upon the island's most beautiful beach, and its chic minimalist designs focus the attention on the lush surroundings. The cerulean

Andaman Sea washes up upon a pristinely white beach and we advise staying in one of their four ultra-luxurious Grand Pool Suites. Don't worry if you never make it into your private Jacuzzi; you'll probably be spending all your time in your own infinity pool, gazing out over the ocean with a Mai Tai in hand. In the morning, take one of the hotel's kayaks out to the middle of the bay for some amazing snorkeling.

Insider's tip? Bring a loaf of bread; you won't believe the plethora of fish that come flocking to you. The world-class Anumba Spa offers a wide range of unmissable treatments, and morning

yoga classes with a panoramic ocean view will ensure that you remain blissfully peaceful long after your treatment has finished. Borrow a couple of bikes to explore the island's verdant landscapes, and come back satisfied that you have found one of the most beautiful spots on earth.

THE NAKA ISLAND A LUXURY COLLECTION RESORT AND SPA

Phuket / *Thailand*

Accessible only by private speedboat, the Naka Island resort offers something that few others can, a genuine sense of seclusion. Yet with the journey from Phuket International Airport taking only 25 minutes it would be a lie to say this comes as a result of endless journeying.

Each of the resort's 67 villas is designed with their surroundings in mind. The natural wood employed throughout frames spectacular views of limestone cliffs, as well as the 'James Bond Island' of Phang Nga Bay. Bordering the structures are tropical gardens, themselves providing a pleasant backdrop to the brilliant open air bathroom. From the moment you set eyes on the infinity pool cascading down

onto the beach it quickly becomes clear that The Naka Island resort has worked diligently on making sure nature is prominent throughout. When it comes to dining the offerings are similarly Thai-centric. Both Tonsai, providing casual all day dining, and My Grill, a grill-house specialising in the freshest seafood and the juiciest southern Thai steaks, are found on the beachside. Z Bar is the perfect spot to sample cocktails while the sun sets on the Andaman Sea.

The Naka Island Spa consists of 12 private treatment suites including four 'couples' suites. Here, outdoor rainforest showers, a private plunge pool, a steam room and steam bed keep you in top condition. Visit the Kanieep pool for

something a little different, where alternate hot and cold pools deliver the ultimate foot massage.

INDIGO **PEARL**

Phuket / Thailand

A visit to Indigo Pearl, a resort blessed by its location between the lush Phuket rainforest and the sparkling shores of the Andaman Ocean, buys you a brief yet memorable share of Thai paradise. The rare wildlife calling the rainforest on this sheltered Northern stretch home, shares unrivalled views out across the ocean with the hotel.

Worth visiting is the incomparable Coqoon Spa, with its Nest treatment centres found nestled in the verdant Phuket rainforest, offers tailored treatments. Black Ginger, the showpiece restaurant floating calmly on the lagoon, a self-proclaimed 'modern masterpiece' of Thai architecture, treats guests to rare southern delicacies. One dish serving minced crab and pork even allows you to 'roll your own' spring rolls!

The resort's design is concentrated on Phuket's heritage as a former tin mining centre. Reclaimed building materials emphasise the deep connection that runs through Indigo Pearl's history. Each unique, secluded Pool Villa at Indigo Pearl offers a stay in the height of luxury. Dense rainforest is the backdrop and private pool the entertainment.

AMANPURI
Phuket / *Thailand*

Amanpuri takes its name from the Sanskrit word meaning 'place of peace' and when you experience what the resort offers this will make complete sense. The pavilions and villa homes are found deep in a coconut plantation, itself on a headland overlooking the Andaman Sea – a location which lends itself to relaxation.

Facilities are designed to reflect the style and elegance of Thai culture. The six high-roofed, wood and glass spa treatment rooms allow light to spill in, while the private-steam room and outdoor meditation sala stay faithful to the nation's heritage. PADI-accredited scuba dive programmes provide quality year-round entertainment and a chance to explore the wide variety of fish and coral reef, even for beginners.

Phuket's Khao Phra Thaeo national park is ideal for elephant trekking through its dense jungle.

The island's cultural offerings are similarly rich – the Talang museum provides a large collection of artefacts from the Moluccas while the 30 Buddhist temples are an interesting diversion.

THE ST. REGIS BANGKOK

Bangkok | Thailand

The first thing you are likely to notice on arrival is the attention paid to you by the renowned St. Regis personal 'butler' service. Escorted to your room, take advantage of the unpacking service they provide so that you can immediately appreciate the vistas offered up by floor-to-ceiling windows.

Another view not to miss is found on the 12th floor Sky Lounge where cocktails are partnered with panoramas of the ever-changing city skyline. Our tip is to head up after the sun sets to truly get the best atmosphere.

Pampering is available from the Elemis Spa, far from the bustling street on the 15th floor. Rasul chambers administer ancient Arabian bathing treatments involving the application of mineral-rich clay and subsequent cleansing

by heat and steam treatment, both working to exfoliate skin and extract toxins.

Choosing from the hotel's of three restaurants and three bars allows for some variation during your stay. Although if the list must be whittled down to one, Jojo, offering rustic Italian cuisine, is a good bet. If you find yourself staying over a weekend, Sunday brunch at VIU overlooking the Royal Bangkok Sports Club is not to be missed.

Exploiting its central location on the Rajadamri Road, the St. Regis Bangkok provides a direct link to the Bangkok Skytrain from its second floor. From here your passage to the city's wide range of businesses, boutiques and restaurants opens up. Similarly accessible is the nearby Lumpini Park where winding lakes host rowing boats and locals practice Tai Chi.

SILAVADEE POOL **SPA RESORT**

Koh Samui / Thailand

A place that offers seclusion, exclusivity and paradise all in one location has finally found its place on Earth. The allure of Thailand has long attracted those seeking more than a dash of adventure, sun and glamour – from backpackers to all out jet-setters- there's something for everyone in this part of the world.

The extraordinary Silavadee Pool Spa Resort (Silavadee means 'beautiful rock' in Thai) prides itself on Thai hospitality. It carries its name well, nestled as it is in the ruggedly beautiful hillside overlooking the hotel's own stretch of sand (known by locals as the 'secret beach').

There are only a handful of pool villas and rooms in this resort, lending it an intimate feel. Elegant guest rooms are sleek in their teak décor and boast private infinity-edge pools and Aqua Jet Massage Bed from which to savour the panoramic views.

There's a unique butler service available 24 hours a day to help you with all and any requests such as recommending restaurants, private island tours, babysitting services or even setting up a private barbeque function -whatever floats your boat!

The Height restaurant serves up first-class cuisine with local and international specialities- try the

various curries and delicately spiced dishes for some authentic and healthy gourmet experiences.

If you crave an escape from the mundanities of everyday urban stress, little can top a holiday in Thailand at the Silavadee Pool Spa Resort.

FUSION **MAIA DA NANG**

Da Nang City / Vietnam

Imagine the scene: an infinity pool surrounded by palm trees looking out to the deep blue ocean and all your spa treatments free! Fusion Maia Da Nang is a place of total serenity and with the largest spa in Vietnam it is the first in Asia to include spa treatments in the cost of guest rooms. Yes, you heard us correctly. Guests can enjoy minimum two pampering sessions each day of their stay at the Maia Spa. The resort created the mantra, "Natural Living Practices," which is a seven-principle guideline on how to achieve a balanced lifestyle. Guests can expect to leave this holiday with a wonderful sense of relaxation.

As you arrive, there's the opportunity to wander through bamboo-lined paths to your private villa that looks out to your own pool and courtyard garden. Inside, Vietnamese inspirations from the Imperial Citadel fuse with contemporary touches for a chic, yet modern atmosphere.

To make guests' stay even more enjoyable, Fusion Maia serves breakfast anytime, anywhere, including in Fusion Lounge in charming Unesco World Heritage town of Hoi An. There are a plethora of options for food, many of them suited to the wellbeing conscious.

To end a day in paradise, be sure to have your camera ready while lazing in the poolside day bed because the sprawling infinity pool reflects the colourful sky and palm trees at sunset - beauty is reflected everywhere here.

PRINCESS D'ÂN NAM RESORT & SPA

Phan Thiet / *Vietnam*

Far from the bustling streets of Ho Chi Minh City lies an Asian paradise named after Princess D'An Nam; a boutique hotel quite unlike any other in Asia.

Guests can hide away in exclusive villas packed with the charms of the ancient orient. They offer panoramic views of lush gardens, designed by renowned landscape artist Alan W. Carle, and the turquoise ocean - not to mention the private plunge pool!

Taking time out at the opulent 1,800 square foot spa is a guest favourite, as skilled hands restore your spirits with soothing ingredients like honey, cloves, coconut oil, golden yellow turmeric, and ylang ylang. The personalized treatments are designed to cater to your specific needs, treating anything from muscular pains to circulatory problems, and everything in between. Designed to resemble an

ancient Greco-Roman temple and taking in views of the sloping sand dunes you'll find it hard not to relax.

When you're not being pampered, there are some unmissable destinations to explore like the Binh Chau Hot Springs and the wildlife of Ta Cu Mountain. Phan Thiet also boasts one of the best golf courses in Vietnam designed by Nick Faldo, the Ocean Dunes Golf Club. With this resort overlooking the East Sea, sand dunes, ranging mountains and red canyons, it would be rude not to take a four-wheel exploration of the area - spectacular mountain rides in vintage jeeps are awe-inspiring.

In the resort's restaurants on-site chefs capture the intricate flavours of Vietnam with local dishes that set the tone for the authentic atmosphere in this remarkable spot.

SHANGRI-LA'S
BORACAY RESORT & SPA
Boracay | *Philippines*

The best-kept secret in the Philippines, Shangri-La's Boracay Resort and Spa is undisputably mesmerizing. This is clear from the moment you set eyes on its white sands and crystal waters while sitting aboard the private speedboat that whisks you away from the airport.

Guests have a choice of 219 rooms, suites and villas which are designed with modern architecture, combined with native touches and tasteful amenities. The villas provide devoted butler service as well as sweeping views of either the sprawling ocean or the lush tropical gardens.

Aside from kayaking and deep-sea diving, you can spend a day of pampering at CHI, The Spa where you can relax and renew the body and spirit. Reserve an intimate tree-top Tuscan dinner at Rima or enjoy drinks at Solana around a fire pit after watching the sunset. A stay at this beachfront sanctuary will make getting back to reality tougher than ever.

THE FULLERTON **HOTEL**

Singapore

Located at the mouth of the Singapore River, the city's historic centre of trade, The Fullerton Hotel exploits its central location to the full. The focal point of commercial activity in its prime; now guests at this iconic luxury hotel can enjoy easy access to the best shopping around, with the Marina Bay Shoppes within easy walking distance.

This is not to say there isn't plenty to keep you entertained within the hotel grounds. Constructed in 1928, the building once home to The General Post Office and The Chamber of Commerce is suitably grand. This is nowhere more abundantly clear than from the lavish 25-metre infinity pool. Sip a cocktail while taking in the towering Doric columns to one side and the Singapore River to the other.

Guests can expect to find a warm welcome inside the hotel with soft vanilla tones and elegant modern touches that complement The Fullerton Hotel's rich heritage. Many rooms feature balconies that open up to reveal beautiful vistas of the city skyline.

Dining offerings include the finest Chinese cuisine from Jade, a restaurant whose walls are decked out in silver and gold. Try the dim sum creations that the restaurant prides itself on. Alternatively, The Lighthouse, an Italian restaurant so named as a nod to the beneficent role it fulfilled early in the previous century, has stunning panoramic views that are matched only by the quality of the food.

Nearby is Boat Quay, an enormously popular dining and entertainment strip. In addition it is well worth making the short journey by underground travelator to see Singapore's national icon, the Merlion, which is particularly spectacular at night.

SHANGRI-LA **SINGAPORE**

Singapore

Take one look at the location of the Shangri-La Hotel and you may think that you'll do well to find a minute's peace; set at the heart of Singapore, with prime access to the best shopping and restaurants there is plenty to keep you entertained. Yet the smile that greets each guest from arrival provides the overriding image of a stay here, and the special service means every moment spent at the hotel is peaceful in itself.

There's space enough to relax after a day in the city and each room's cutting edge design draws from Asian culture, with many taking in stunning city vistas. Enjoy the 15 acres of lush tropical gardens for which the hotel is famed.

Guests can certainly expect to be well-fed. The Nadaman group of restaurants has been serving quality local specialities since 1830, and rightly prides itself on the fine Kaiseki offerings. The spectacular Waterfall Café lies at the heart of tropical gardens and boasts a wine list that takes in premier vintages from across the globe.

139

W SINGAPORE **SENTOSA COVE**

Singapore

Singapore: it glitters through the hazy night-time sky, a beacon of old meets new, of East meets West. The towering skyscrapers reaching greedily up towards the clouds are tempered by modest mosques and serene Buddhist temples. W Hotels, a name synonymous with being the last line in modern luxury, has finally flung open the doors of the newest addition to its fleet in this timeless locale: the W Singapore Sentosa Cave, a construction of contemporary, chic luxury. Located on an exclusive island resort fitted with personal berths, the W Singapore is almost painfully cool. Gaze out over the marina as you sip a devilishly delicious Singapore Sling on your balcony, or relax on one of the glowing daybeds by the pool. Later, cool off by slipping into your sunken bath, the darkly calming flint walls and lush orchids providing welcome relief from the blazing Malaysian sun. The AWAY Spa is a measure of effortless indulgence that is simply not to be missed. You'll be forgiven for never wanting to leave this haven of stylish escapism.

THE FULLERTON **BAY HOTEL**

Singapore

The Fullerton Bay Hotel was designed to celebrate the city's rich heritage with polished rosewood surfaces and latticed screens that create the most authentic of atmospheres. Natural palettes pay testament to the old adage that simplicity is found at the heart of perfection, with crowning touches of elegance applied by leather and chrome fittings.

With only one 100 rooms, each with a private balcony and full-length windows, you're unlikely to feel crowded. Everything on view at The Fullerton Bay Hotel merely adds further weight to the praise heaped on famed designer Andre Fu.

Guests are well-set for dining at The Fullerton Bay Hotel, with Clifford's library of wine a perfect accompaniment to the views of Marina Bay, captured through ten-metre high floor-to-ceiling windows. Make sure to visit Lantern, a rooftop bar that sets the standard for style. Taking its name from the red lanterns that used to hang from the pier to guide boats into port, the bar is a veritable honey pot for guests seeking to catch sight of the Singapore cityscape from a new angle – and with a drink in hand!

If visitors can pull themselves from the hotel, they'll find a host of top attractions virtually on their doorstep. The world's tallest Ferris wheel, the Singapore Flyer, and the beautiful Gardens by the Bay offer the perfect photo opportunities at sunset. Those after a spot of culture will have their appetites well sated after a visit to any or all of the Asian Civilizations Museum, Singapore Art Museum and Esplanade – Theatres on the Bay.

ST. REGIS **BALI RESORT**

Bali : Indonesia

The St. Regis Bali Resort is a unique hotel experience. This all-suite and villa resort is a destination within itself, giving the guests the option of staying exclusively on the premises. There is a 24-hour butler service that caters to your every need—whether it is a freshly pressed suit for the morning or a last-minute gift for a loved one.

The resort is located on the stunning soft white sand beachfront of Nusa Dua, combining panoramic views of the Indian ocean with lush, vibrant Balinese gardens and 3500sqm of salt water, lagoon, safe to swim in.

There is a broad selection of world-class cuisine available, with three dining venues and a variety of resources available to every guest. These include private rooms for events or meetings, a

beachfront wedding chapel; the Remede Spa, a fitness centre and a children's learning centre.

Because of the attentive staff and convenience of the resort, you can spend all of your time lounging by the lagoon pool and making the most of the exceptional surroundings.

THE MULIA - NUSA DUA, BALI

Bali | Indonesia

Balinese culture is suffused with colour, art, religion and natural beauty; its people are so friendly that it's impossible to not be seduced by the atmosphere on this island. The Mulia (a respected member of Preferred Hotels and Resorts) encapsulates all of these qualities with a stunning all-suite series of properties. Offering 111 ultra high-end, sparkling new suites, together with private Jacuzzi on the balcony and personal butler service, book a stay at the properties and you're bound to remember the experience for quite some time.

Picture yourself just steps from the white sandy beach. Wander down to the sea, or meander through private pathways that lead to secluded gardens filled with the vibrant colours of nature's finest blooms. The resort's pool and beach are stunning and immaculate. The exclusive Nusa Dua area stretches over 30 hectares, taking in over one kilometre of ranging beaches.

The comfortable and intimate suites are decked out with state-of-the art amenities and elegant furnishings. Food lovers are in for a healthy treat with some exciting selections to keep things interesting. Any one of the restaurants, bars or deli has a unique ambiance so you can relax with afternoon tea or plump straight for early evening cocktails. At night, one of the bars transforms into an incredibly stylish venue for the fashionable crowd. Grasp the chance to get hands on with Balinese culture and take up the dance lessons that are so filled with colour.

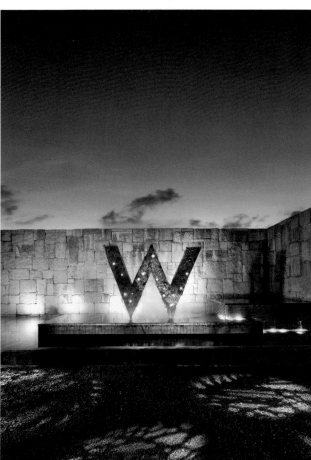

W RETREAT & SPA BALI – SEMINYAK

Bali / Indonesia

W Retreat & Spa Bali – Seminyak only opened in March 2011 but has already made an impression on the Island of the Gods. Contemporary and cutting-edge, with a fun, relaxed vibe, this uber-chic retreat is Bali's trendiest enclave.

Vibrantly designed with the latest modcons, yet luxurious and comfortable, the retreats and villas are private sanctuaries that you will never want to leave...you actually don't have to! It is, however, worth dragging yourself out of your ultra-comfortable, signature W bed for the breakfast experience: an endless feast of delights from fresh tropical juices to gourmet coffees; pastries to pancakes; eggs cooked to your personal liking and that's not even starting on the cold meat and cheeses; the sushi and sashimi!

After such a hearty start to the day, you'll probably fancy a doze on a daybed by the tropical-feel pool. You need never move from this spot all day: the friendly W team are on hand to ensure you don't have to lift a finger, regularly supplying snacks (more food!) and sun cream.

There's a gym if you really feel the need to burn off some of those breakfast calories, but holidays are all about relaxing and indulgence so treat yourself to a treatment at the 24-hour spa instead (yes, you can massage at midnight!)

As you would expect from a W Retreat, the evening vibe is fun and funky. Mingle over a martini at sunset against an audible backdrop of DJ beats before cosying up in a "lobster-

trap" booth (once you see, it you'll understand) at Starfish Bloo – don't miss the crispy duck salad!

AMANKILA

Bali / *Indonesia*

Amidst the rambling verdure of this paradise island lies Bali's Amankila Resort, set atop the dramatic cliffs overlooking the serene Lombok Strait. This hotel epitomises luxurious tranquillity; no wonder so many high profile personalities choose anonymity and peace here. You can expect a unique type of holistic relaxation and an ultra-discreet atmosphere.

Each thatched villa's chic décor is influenced by local traditional architecture and is wonderfully secluded by the groves or fragrant bougainvillea and frangipani trees that cloak the island. You can unwind with complimentary, twice-weekly yoga sessions –or arrange your own private classes – under the coconut groves, or enjoy the Indonesian afternoon tea served at the hotel's stunning three-tiered infinity pool. A full spa menu offers an immense range of lush treatments for anyone in need of further pampering.

Gourmets are in for a treat as Amankila offers a number of incredible dining experiences. From private Balinese feasts to their incredible sunset satay experience, every second is one to be cherished in this Eden-like retreat.

147

QUALIA

Hamilton Island, Great Barrier Reef | Australia

qualia, meaning "a collection of deeper sensory experiences" in Latin, is a precise indication of the experience you can expect during your stay at this resort. From the moment you arrive at qualia staff create an ambience that caters to your personalized needs.

qualia is situated on the secluded northern-most tip of Hamilton Island and is surrounded by all the splendour of the Great Barrier Reef. This resort features 60 uniquely designed pavilions that flow through to private sundecks, some with infinity plunge pools, overlooking the sea. There are an assortment of authentically Australian, relaxing treatments at the spa, and both casual and fine dining choices on-site for guests to indulge in.

The subtly elegant and uniquely Australian décor of qualia effortlessly brings the outdoors in, fusing the

property with the peaceful beauty of the Australian Eucalyptus and turquoise waters of the surrounding Whitsunday Islands. The mesmerizing calm will make your stay here a truly memorable one.

BLANKET BAY **LUXURY LODGE**

Otago / *New Zealand*

An elegant but rustic lodge lies in a place idyllic enough for the filming of the Lord of the Rings trilogy. The breathtaking Blanket Bay Luxury Lodge overlooks a crystal clear lake, with sprawling mountains as a backdrop.

There are six intimate Lodge Rooms and seven suites, all filled with sumptuous furnishings, plush rugs and a high timber ceiling and, in the suites, there are even open fireplaces, making for a cosy log cabin feel. Expect only the highest quality of service as well.

A mere 45 minutes from Queenstown, the adventure capital of the world, you'll be tempted to go fly-fishing or even heli-skiing - if you dare!

A frequent guest, 'Gandalf' from Lord of the Rings, asked in the lodge's guest book, 'Who needs an after-life when there is Paradise on Earth?' So join Gandalf and Frodo for a holiday that's more than other-wordly.

EAGLES **NEST**
Bay of Islands / *New Zealand*

Nestled on top of a private peninsula overlooking New Zealand's Bay of Islands is the ultra-contemporary resort, Eagles Nest. This North Island boutique retreat is made up of five exclusive villas so you don't have to worry about crowds by the pool or at dinner.

All are perfectly appointed with spacious living areas and heated horizon edged pool, gourmet kitchen and a fabulous cinema system. You could be forgiven for never leaving your own private paradise so should you dream of a poolside barbecue or a nine-course dinner in-villa prepared by fabulous resident chefs, nothing is too much trouble for the exclusive concierge team.

Guests can explore 75 acres of sub-tropical native bush with secluded beaches and more than 144 islands. No one leaves disappointed, so enjoy a bird's eye view of absolute paradise—you won't forget it in a hurry.

CONTENTS THE AMERICAS

Canada

United States

Mexico

Caribbean

Brazil

Chile

Argentina

FAIRMONT **PACIFIC RIM**

Vancouver / *Canada*

With unobstructed views of the harbour and mountains and a prime location adjacent to the Cruise Ship terminal, Fairmont Pacific Rim in Vancouver stands proud in an area rich in history and culture. The hotel is located at the heart of the historic port and financial district with the stunning backdrop of the North Shore Mountains, Stanley Park and Coal Harbour offering unrivalled views.

Sophisticated and cosmopolitan, welcoming and contemporary; Fairmont Pacific Rim combines the best of Asia and the Pacific Northwest in its layout and décor.

Food lovers can delight in ORU - featuring food of the Pacific Northwest with flavours of the Pacific Rim; giovane – an Italian-inspired café and wine bar, and the Lobby Lounge features live entertainment six nights a week.

Fairmont Pacific Rim prides itself on taking five-star standards to new heights. There are 377 rooms (with a boutique experience) all lavishly appointed with naturally inspired materials, comfortable furnishings and state-of-the-art technology. Looking to relax? Enjoy the Willow Stream spa, full fitness centre, outdoor terrace with Jacuzzis and

meditation pods with a wonderful rooftop pool and private cabanas and fire pits.

Lovers of the great outdoors are in for a treat with access to golf, ski slopes and sailing boats all in the same day! Shopping addicts and culture vultures are equally well served with a plethora of superb boutiques and world-class theatre performances just a stone's throw away.

157

SPARKLING HILL **RESORT**

Vernon / *Canada*

Perched on a ridge with awe-inspiring views of Lake Okanagan and the Monashee and Pinnacle Mountains lies the magnificent Sparkling Hill Resort. A stay here literally sparkles with elegance.

The property boasts 3.5 million Swarovski crystals in virtually every element of the property. It is the first public building in the world with crystal architecture.

Enjoy spotting bald eagles, hawks, and deer as you walk along the surrounding trails. Guests can also experience fine dining at the lavish PeakFine restaurant, with dramatic sunset views over Lake Okanagan. Equally impressive is Fireside Lounge, where lucky guests can admire the wonders of a crystal ceiling firsthand.

Both captivating and contemplative, Sparkling Hill possesses a one-of-a-kind, multi-faceted beauty

that is unparalleled in North America. Come to experience the charm of crystal architecture, but we warn you that the rest of the world may seem a bit dull in comparison after your stay here.

CLAYOQUOT **WILDERNESS RESORT**

Vancouver Island / *Canada*

Your first glimpse of Clayoquot Wilderness Resort comes after a short flight from Vancouver, across a string of snow-covered peaks and down into a valley of waterfalls, before touching down as a bear cub races across the field. As soon as you stepped off the plane, you'll be greeted by managing directors, John and Adele, with a warm smile and a firm handshake. Right from the start, you know Clayoquot is not like other resorts. It's a family run establishment so you feel as though you've been exclusively welcomed into someone's luxury home.

With only 20 luxury tents in total, linked together by cedar boardwalks along the river's estuary, Clayoquot promises intimacy. Here there are unexpected comforts in a remote wilderness and you'll find sanctuary in the great white canvas prospector-style tents. You can lose yourself in the resort's lounge tents (the games and the library tents); their plush turn-of-the-century dark polished woods echo old, familiar Gentlemen's Clubs. Warm and inviting, modern amenities are disguised within beautiful, antique furnishings.

Specializing in remarkable activities, you can find paradise while hiking across miles of unspoilt nature or watch whales in the rolling waves of the Pacific Ocean. A favourite with the guests at Clayoquot is horseback riding – with a great stable of horses, talented riders and beginners are in for a treat. What started with a handshake will conclude with hugs and kisses (and a tear) as you reluctantly leave the resort at the end of your stay.

THE **CHATWAL**
New York City / USA

Any trip to New York City should include a stay at The Chatwal. This extraordinary hotel fuses Art Deco that cleverly showcases New York's past with the luxury accommodation of today. Master architect, Thierry Despont, beautifully restored this landmark building, overlooking no detail and sparing no expense.

Because of this, the Chatwal offers a comforting and peaceful escape from the hurried environment of Times Square. Guests can spend their time at the fitness centre or relaxing at the Elizabeth Arden Red Door Spa. Even the in-room amenities speak of the Chatwal's commitment to quality – Aprey shampoos and conditioners are the little touches that guests really appreciate.

After a day spent relaxing within the hotel you can indulge in the cuisine of top NY chef, Geoffrey Zakarian, at the Lambs Club Restaurant and prohibition cocktails at The Lambs Club Bar. No matter what you choose to do, The Chatwal is in the perfect location to enjoy the city and then escape it.

THE **PLAZA**

New York City | *USA*

The Plaza Hotel is as integral to New York's landscape as Central Park whose boundary it so elegantly flanks. Standing proud at the entrance of the city's greenest gateway, it continues to attract the world's most glamorous visitors and has done so since it opened its doors in 1907. Having recently undergone transformations, it nevertheless retains its world-famous, timeless charm - further enhanced through the addition of its modern amenities.

Each of the distinctive suites offer 24 hour butler service, which can be controlled through an iPad stored in each room. All self-respecting spa buffs must make a stop at the hotel's Caudalie Vinotherapie Spa where specialized treatments place the onus on fruit acids and their beneficial effect in rejuvenating the skin. There is of course an excellently appointed Fitness Center, La Palestra,

and the Warren-Tricomi Salon is the perfect spot for a cut and blow dry before hitting the town.

The in-house evening entertainment promises a classy end to the day, with The Champagne Bar providing the meanest cocktails and The Rose Club live jazz on Wednesdays and Thursdays. Highly recommended is Afternoon Tea at The Palm Court (some of the finest cakes, patisseries and tea blends imaginable) - a nod to the elegant grandeur of yesteryear with a modern twist on the menu.

One thing is certain: one night and day at The Plaza and you'll feel like you're on the set of F.Scott Fitzgerald's The Great Gatsby - and you are!

MANDARIN ORIENTAL **NEW YORK**
New York City / *USA*

Found at the top of the Time Warner Centre, a booking at the Mandarin Oriental New York guarantees you breathtaking views of Central Park and the Hudson River. A brief walk finds you exploring Fifth Avenue boutiques, experiencing the Broadway Theatre magic or leaves you awestruck by the bright lights of Times Square.

The five-star spa provides top level treatments from its bamboo, stone and gold leaf rooms while the 75-foot indoor lap pool means you can keep in shape after the previous day's indulgences.

Asiate, the 35th floor restaurant offers stunning views from its floor to ceiling windows. Designed by the world-renowned Tony Chi it features as its focal point a sparkling tree branch hanging from the ceiling, symbolising wintry Central Park trees.

Local ingredients take prominence, with menus passing in time with the seasons. Asiate's award winning wall of wine holds up to 2,500 bottles, making up what is quite possibly the most extraordinary collection anywhere in the world.

ST. REGIS **NEW YORK**

New York City / *USA*

To get a true sense of what New York is all about, you need to stay in the heart of the action. The St Regis New York prescribes to this way of thinking too; exploiting a prime location which boasts world-famous attractions within easy walking distance of its illustrious premises.

Sample the delights of Broadway, Central Park and Fifth Avenue shopping before returning to a warm cup of tea or a fine whiskey at the Thornwillow at the hotel. Posited as 'the city's best kept secret' by the hotel, this tranquil boutique on the ground floor means you can slow the pace whenever the city threatens to get too hectic.

Be sure also to drop by the King Cole Bar, where the wall is adorned by American painter Maxfield Parrish's 30-foot-wide, century-old King Cole

masterpiece. This tasteful backdrop decorates the bar said to have been witness to the Bloody Mary's arrival (and enhancement!) in America.

The 164 guest rooms and 65 suites feature residential elegance with lavish furnishings, marble bathrooms and plush signature St. Regis beds. The St. Regis New York also boasts one of a kind designer suites – the Dior Suite, the Tiffany Suite and the Bentley Suite – with inspired decor that captures the essence of these luxury brands.

The Remède Spa at St. Regis makes sure tailored treatments relax tight muscles - aided in no small part by the champagne on offer. Personal trainers at the Fitness Centre keep you in shape no matter how excessive your New York diet, or if all this exercise seems a

little too strenuous, yoga or Pilates instructors are available for one-on-one sessions.

THE SETAI **MIAMI BEACH**

Miami / *USA*

The Setai, Miami Beach has the privilege of sitting on one of the most widely desirable beach-side fronts in one of the most exciting cities on the planet. This is a 5-star hotel that has more than a few surprises up its sleeve. Something of a scene-stealer, it's easy to see why you would be seduced by this landmark establishment; a canny blend of Asian and European styles. Elegantly sandwiched as it is between the relative serenity of its white sandy beaches, the hectic buzz of the city's social scene and the historic Art Deco district, you could be forgiven for thinking that you're in for a noisy ride. Think again - the

moment you step into the lobby and start to explore this extraordinary space with its Zen ambiance, its intimate, cosy corners and well-conceived scents and sounds, the hustle and bustle of the city melts clean away. It's the best of both worlds; party-goers have Miami on their doorstep while those in need of peace and quiet need never leave the building.

The guest suites would give any of the sumptuous privately-owned homes in this glamorous area a run for their money. There's no room for ostentation however. The Setai is all about clean lines and airy

spaces in a décor that combines black granite and teak with crisp whites. Art Deco has been central to this part of the coast since the 1930's and this building has been well-preserved since its beginnings as the fames Dempsey Vanderbilt Hotel. Textures are rich; materials are natural with a heavy use of wood, brick and slate framed by tastefully presented fresh flowers and sound absorbing oriental carpets. Healthy living is taken seriously in a city where people work and play hard. There are three fabulous pools, perfect for catching the sun and making the most of the outstanding pool bar food as well as the hotel's private beach. For relaxing indulgence and pampering, the Asian-inspired Spa at The Setai delivers ancient rituals of treatment.

Food lovers are well catered for as you would expect. The Sunday Brunch here is renowned with an impressive selection of tasty and fresh dishes to sample. For the ultimate culinary treat, be sure to book a table at The Restaurant which boasts an exhibition kitchen where guests can witness the process of 'creative Asian cuisine' first hand. Waiting staff are more than happy to guide you through; making for a truly interactive dining experience.

If you are looking for something that will blow your mind with a money-no-object experience try the 10,000sq ft Penthouse. Available on request only of course, this extraordinary penthouse boasts sweeping wrap-around balconies with 360-degree views of Miami's stunning skyline. The four bedrooms, music lounge, kitchen and dining room complete with a private wine cellar collection make this the world's premier luxury hotel suite.

Meanwhile down below and a few blocks away, the glittering lights of Ocean Drive and Lincoln Road beckon enticingly with their world-class boutiques, cafes, restaurants, music and vibrant culture.

THE BETSY **SOUTH BEACH**

Miami Beach | *USA*

The Betsy is a distinguished landmark in a town where flamboyance is generally the order of the day. The hotel stands proud on Ocean Drive along Miami's South Beach and behind its colonial facade lies a haven of peace with just 61 tasteful and understated rooms and suites.

For a creative touch and sensory details, you're in for a treat here. Fresh orchids grace every room while the inspirational design marries contemporary style and state-of-the-art technology with elegant touches of yesteryear.

There are stunning ocean views from the rooms which beg for a trip to the beach. A courtyard pool sits off of the airy lobby in an atmosphere that is quintessential 'salon'. From floor to ceiling, Betsy offers an

intimate retreat from the coastline with tasteful splashes of traditional colonial splendour.

The Deck at The Betsy is an expansive rooftop with sweeping views of the Atlantic adorned with palm trees. A Zen-inspired calm comes through with natural materials like wood decking, stone and bamboo all shielded by retractable sails. The Wellness Spa offers treatments, therapies and yoga in a location that's therapeutic in itself.

While away the hours on the rooftop with speciality cocktails, light meals at the lobby bar, or go for Laurent Tourondel's refined take on the iconic American steakhouse. You'll be dreaming of your time at The Betsy far from the madding crowd for a long time to come – and planning your next visit.

W **SOUTH BEACH**

Miami / *USA*

W South Beach prides itself on its location at the heart of the Miami buzz. That's why each suite is carefully tailored to tap into the best aspects of the city's vibrant atmosphere, combining the height of chic design with sharp little touches every discerning guest will appreciate.

Whether it's the luxurious bathrooms, the balcony or the extraordinary ocean views you're likely to find plenty of reasons to fall in love with your room. This is not to say there aren't plenty of pulls within the hotel grounds. Explore the Grove and its lush gardens to spend some quality time with the ones you love. The serenity lends itself to reflecting on the highlights of an unforgettable journey.

Take advantage of the 'beach ambassadors' who gladly show you to the best sunbathing spot

on the beach. Be warned, though, as the hours quickly flit away. Over 7000 sq. feet of spa await those seeking a different kind of relaxation. We personally recommend paying a visit to the Beach bar, which offers the chance to rest within sight and sound of the Atlantic's golden coast. Cocktails have rarely tasted better than those sipped here and drinks accompanied by the setting sun really do provide a story to tell upon your return home.

When it's time to feed the hunger that the day has worked up, dine out at Mr Chow where the finest Asian cuisine is on show. These offerings are rivalled only by The Dutch, the showcase restaurant that prides itself on its American heritage – hailing from New York it provides some of the country's classics.

BLANTYRE

Massachusetts / *USA*

Blantyre is the hotel of choice for anyone looking for a stay that feels more like your family's country house than a hotel. It combines the comfort of home with the romantic elegance of eras long past. Beginning with the drive through a sprawling 115-acre property to the initial view of the charming cottages, one can anticipate the comfortable atmosphere awaiting them behind the leaded windows.

At Blantyre, no detail has been overlooked. Every room is filled with delightfully overstuffed chairs and fresh cut flowers. Wall to wall fabrics and floral patterns give an added level of sophistication and romance.

Throughout the 115 acres you can take part in a variety of outdoor activities that range from tennis and croquet in the summer or ice skating and snowshoeing in the winter. Or if you prefer lounging over physical activities you can also enjoy a day at their renowned spa—quaintly called The Potting Shed and open until "whenever."

Dining on the estate is just as decadent as the décor and spa treatments. They have won many awards for their dining experience and selection of wine. In addition they are a member of Relais and Chateaux hotel group and the wine cellar has been awarded Wine Spectators prestigious Grand Award consecutively since 2009.

This can become a delightful retreat for one person or the entire family since you're able to rent out the entire property for private events. With 21 individually decorated rooms, it is the perfect destination for a quaint and peaceful wedding. Or you could stay 21 times to experience each of the rooms for yourself.

COLONY **PALMS**

Palm Springs / *USA*

Colony Palms is a beautiful fusion of old Hollywood glamour and modern design. Recently restored by Martyn Lawrence-Bullard, a renowned architectural designer, this luxury boutique hotel is an ideal destination for anyone looking to escape to a world of glamour and decadence.

The architecture and design of Colony Palms is reflective of the Spanish design found throughout other areas of southern California. The combination of culture, style, and sophistication make this resort truly unique.

Guests can dine at the Purple Palm, one of the most popular restaurants in Palm Springs and real destination for gourmets. You are also only moments from one of the most glamorous areas of Southern California where there is plenty of shopping and dining to enjoy.

HOTEL **ESENCIA**

Riviera Maya | Mexico

Imagine waking to the sound of waves crashing onto the shore on one of the most beautiful beaches on the Riviera Maya. It sounds too good to be true but it is solid reality at the seaside estate, Esencia. This lavish hotel offers awe-inspiring horizons, two swimming pools, a personalized butler service and a gourmet restaurant among others. You're treated like royalty by charming staff who remember your name and favourite drink as soon as you arrive.

There are but a handful of ocean and garden view guest rooms, suites and cottages of which two thirds have private pools. The feel is intimate and exclusive. Twelve-foot high ceilings and mahogany louvered doors open up to colourful tropical gardens and sea views beyond.

Dining at Esencia is also a memorable experience. The chef practices his sophisticated skills on fresh local ingredients to create dishes that are simple, but staggeringly elegant with the finest seafood, meats and fresh salads from this part of the world.

As if you needed any more peace and serenity, there's Aroma; the first organic spa on the Riviera Maya to use pure indigenous fruits, plants and herbs -many of these plants are plucked straight from the hotel's own garden. With nothing but the sea breeze to disturb, an afternoon in the capable hands of professional technicians using ancient Mayan techniques to revitalize body and soul is an absolute must!

Esencia introduces guests to the Mayan world and the best that Mexico has to offer. We won't blame you for postponing your return flight.

CUIXMALA

Careyes / *Mexico*

Originally the private estate of Sir James Goldsmith, this expanse of idyllic beaches and mysterious lagoons is the ideal destination for those craving tranquility. The lush vegetation that surrounds Cuixmala is a haven for exotic animals and thousands of birds. Take a boat tour around the lagoon and spot zebras, white tail deer and coati mundis. With three private beaches, and surfing, diving and fishing opportunities too, you'll never want to get out of the blue water. Luckily, the gracious Cuixmala staff barbeque fresh seafood right on the beach so you'll never have to!

The accommodation is plush ranging from the palatial Casa La Loma to the cosy Casitas perfect for families or groups of friends. For tranquillity and stunning ocean views, the luxurious Casa La Loma and the three glorious villas will tick all the boxes. From splash pool size Jacuzzis and tropical gardens with a private beach to cooks, butlers, and acres of space for families, you'll want for nothing.

The location is home to the ecologically important Chamela-Cuixmala Biosphere Reserve as well as being ideal for surfing, hiking trails, horse riding lessons, scuba diving, boat trips and something truly special - Cuixmala's Turtle Protection Program. This is a rare and unforgettable opportunity to assist in the protection of the Giant Sea Turtles who lay their eggs in the sands of Playa Cuixmala. Staff collects the eggs, removing them from danger from poachers and other predators, and releases the baby turtles into the sea again. Memories to stay with you forever...

NECKER ISLAND

British Virgin Islands

Necker Island is, in a word (or three), simply beyond compare. As the private island home of Sir Richard Branson, it is fitting that this jewel-like haven in the British Virgin Islands should be the epitome of Caribbean bliss. Comprised of 74 acres of alabaster beaches and lush verdure, Necker Island is an unparalleled tropical sanctuary. Factor in its staff of 60, two floodlit tennis courts, and an on-site spa (not to mention its resident flock of flamingos and family of lemurs), and Necker Island is undisputedly the reigning king of holiday bliss. The residences include Temple House (Branson's personal home), the (charmingly named) Love Temple, the four-bedroom luxury catamaran Necker Belle, and six individual one-bedroom Bali Houses, and can accommodate up to 28 friends and loved ones. Rent the island in its entirety to experience consummate tranquillity, or book rooms on an individual basis during the selected Celebration

Weeks, to experience a slice of private island paradise. Fun and relaxation is always on the agenda on Necker Island, dine on your personal favourite dishes or let the team of chefs showcase their own flair. Explore the brilliant surrounding reefs and indulge in private sailing or kite surfing lessons.

AMANYARA

Providenciales / *Turks and Caicos Islands*

Prepare to be dazzled upon entering the Amanyara as its large reception pavilion opens onto an impressive central reflecting pond surrounded by regal mahogany trees. This exquisite spot located in the Turks and Caicos is surrounded by exquisite natural beauty. The Amanyara lives up to its name, which is derived from Sanskrit meaning "peaceful place," and landing here is much like stepping into heaven.

While visiting, guests have the options of staying in pavilions or villas depending on their personal preference. Pavilions overlook tranquil ponds or the oceanfront, and guests should pay particular attention to the newly added pool pavilions that open onto an infinity-edge swimming pool. Villas also look out to tranquil lakes or oceanfront with various amenities, such as a personal cook, housekeeper and four-seat golf buggies.

The dining areas all boast unrivalled ocean views and fine local and Asian cuisine. The bar is a must-see; circular in design and featuring a fantastic soaring ceiling. Leading from the bar is a spacious terrace that is ideal for watching the sunset or for having an after-dinner cigar or nightcap. For those looking to explore the natural wonders of the islands, Amanyara's new Nature Discover Centre employs a full-time naturalist to educate guests of all ages and is the perfect place to go hiking, diving, and snorkelling. Staying at the Amanyara is all about turning off the stress and tuning into nature on your own time. Not a tough call in a place such as this.

PARROT CAY **BY COMO**

Providenciales / *Turks and Caicos Islands*

Untouched diving reefs and deep turquoise sea surround the mile-long, 1000-acre island home of Parrot Cay, a private island resort. Here the sands are a bristling white and the birdlife rich.

Suites and villas come with private pools while specially designed rooms allow natural light to spill from wall to wall. Many of the accommodations come with direct beach access.

For guests seeking even more privacy, there is Parrot Cay Estates, a group of privately owned, rentable three- and five-bedroom homes that come with their own concealed stretch of beach, all within a five-minute buggy ride from the main hotel. Each property is styled in neutral colours that complement the resort's beachfront setting.

The resort's COMO Shambhala Retreat provides guests with top-quality spa treatments, which incorporate nature

into the setting. Elsewhere in the resort, we like the chilled atmosphere that pervades the poolside Lotus restaurant, serving light Caribbean meals in the day and switching to contemporary Asian by night.

CAP **JULUCA**

Anguilla / *British West Indies*

Cap Juluca overlooks a long crescent beach on the British West Indies Island of Anguilla that stretches almost a mile from one corner of the resort to the other. It's a glorious panorama of brilliant white sands and crystal clear waters as far as the eye can see.

The resort is made up of 14 separate Moorish-style beachfront villas. The spacious rooms offer breathtaking ocean views with direct beach access, and there are even six private pool villas. Expect to be well looked after throughout the day from the comfort of your beach lounger, as waiters obligingly ply you with chilled towels, fruit, sorbet and pastries.

After the beach, meander your way to the Wellness Center where the professional therapists have a knack for making their clients feel like the most important person on earth. All services are rooted in indigenous traditions that are tailored to rejuvenate the body and mind – perfect for unwinding after a long flight.

If you have had too much sunbathing for one day, (if that is even possible) take a water taxi to a secluded little bay for some snorkeling over a magnificent coral reef. Just don't forget your underwater camera!

Besides beach and spa treatments, treat yourself to a round of golf on the Championship Golf Course on Anguilla; designed by golf legend Greg Norman and first opened in 2006 it is a much-loved course for golf enthusiasts.

CANOUAN **RESORT**

The Grenadines / *West Indies*

Canouan Resort & the Grenadines Estate Villas lie at the heart of The Grenadines in the south-eastern Caribbean, 20 minutes from Barbados and St Lucia. Everything about this resort spells relaxation as it covers two-thirds of the island essentially making it a private island with lagoons and secluded surroundings. A collection of stunning two to seven bedroom villas offer guests private pools and are dotted with hidden coves and beautiful white beaches. Coral reefs provide excellent diving spots and there are plenty of water sports as well as tennis and golf with a stunning 18-hole championship golf course regarded as

one of the best in the world. The view from the 13th hole is particularly spectacular. Elsewhere, the four signature restaurants offer a great choice of fine cuisine and your wine will be chilled and served to perfection. The team of attentive staff pride themselves on the ultimate personalised service for each and every guest - your glass will never be empty by the pool and they'll remember your name. The 24-hour concierge service see to it that every detail goes to plan so you can just get on with enjoying your holiday to the full. When booking a suite or Villa you can include a Jet transfer, in true James Bond style, to the resort on weekends

for every seven-night stay. Be sure to visit Tobago Cays as well as book a treatment at the Canouan Resort Spa for full on indulgence during your stay.

TXAI **RESORT**

Itacaré / *Brazil*

Although the thought of being suspended midair may make you uneasy, The Txai Resort Itacare will have you literally floating in paradise. The architecture, inspired by the old cocoa plantation houses, is a successful blend of charm and rustic Bahia appeal that seamlessly integrates nature with the buildings. The collection of bungalows suspended on a stilt construction and built over a wooden terrace offers a romantic space - encapsulating an authentic bucolic luxury, with thatched roofing, spacious verandahs, king size beds and a

stunning outdoor shower area that is totally private. A wander round the sleepy town of Itacare is great for gaining a sense of genuine Bahia culture. You can mingle with the friendly locals as they go about their business and while away the evening with some good, traditional dancing.

For resting your jaded body and mind, we think there's no other way to spend an afternoon than to take in the view on a lounge chair, sip on some coconut water while taking the occasional refreshing dip in the plunge pool.

To revive your body after your beach and jungle adventures, head to the Shamash Healing Space. This hill-top spa offers the full range of massage and beauty treatments and therapies for some seriously professional pampering

Although the Txai Resort is the ideal honeymoon or anniversary get-away, the Txai Resort is accommodating to families as well. The resort has separate children's pools and extensive menus tailored to them, on top of babysitting facilities.

Breakfast and dinner are served in the Bahian-style restaurant under a high thatched roof by the beach, or on the candlelit terrace. Lunch is served down by the pool (unless it is raining hard in which case chef and waiters decamp to the restaurant). As you contemplate the setting it's worth planning an expedition to the Atlantic Forest that can be organized by your butler service. Don't leave without discovering the secret waterfalls, wild beaches, mangroves and local craftwork that make the experience of staying at Txai Resort Itacaré so memorable. The most memorable example of how luxury and nature can live together in perfect harmony...

POUSADA ESTRELA **D'ÁGUA**

Trancoso / *Brazil*

Pousada Estrela D'Água delivers a unique strand of luxury.

Located in the village of Trancoso, this is the place to be for some colourful Brazilian culture. Bordered by mangroves alive with exotic birds and flowers and flanked by the white sands of Nativos Beach, this charming little hotel blends seamlessly into its natural surroundings. Rooms feature wooden furnishings and crisp white linen; the Master Suites have a private Jacuzzi or swimming pool whilst the Suites have private terraces with a hammock.

Estrela D'Água offers an authentic gastronomic experience. The menu has many options, from international cuisine to contemporary cuisine from Bahia. There are two restaurants, servicing guests at the beach or in the swimming pool.

Not to be missed are the hotel's organised diving expeditions and kayak tours through the mangroves, and for a truly unforgettable experience, take a boat trip to watch the whales playing in the Atlantic before they start their migratory journey. Golfers enjoy special green-fee rates at the Terravista Course adjacent to the hotel. Arguably Latin America's best golf course, it extends up to the Trancoso cliffs, where the ocean views are unmissable. After such an eventful day, it's time to enjoy a complimentary foot bath, followed by an invigorating treatment at the hotel's spa. Finally, sip a fruit caipirinha and relax as the glowing sun sets on the never-ending horizon.

DPNY **BEACH HOTEL**
Ilhabela *Brazil*

DPNY Beach Hotel sits on the Brazilian island of Ilhabela ('beautiful island' in Portuguese), only 190 kms from São Paulo International Airport. Given the enormous popularity of this region, a stay here is a welcome and relaxing break and comes as a wonderful surprise. Aside from the peaceful ambiance, there is great attention to detail with hand-picked exclusive and trendy art pieces dotted throughout the hotel, inspired by the hippie and chic; resulting in a successful blend of romantic, glamorous and innovation.

Guests are well-catered for at the Beach Club which is considered as being one of the best in South America. There's plenty of fun and adventure here so try your hand at stand up paddling, kayaking, kite-surfing, diving, wakeboarding or book a motor boat ride for some thrills. DPNY's signature Hippie Chic Sangria is a favourite with guests as is Troia Restaurant which offers up top-class dishes ranging from deliciously fresh sushi, oysters, and Mediterranean cuisine.

KENOA **RESORT**

Alagoas / Brazil

A tropical utopia may seem like a bit of an exaggeration, but there is no better way to describe Kenoa Resort. Located on the sandy beaches of the Barra de São Miguel, the resort overlooks the turquoise Atlantic set against lush coconut groves and rugged cliffs. Coupled with clement weather year-round and exclusive access, it's no surprise that this gem is a jealously-kept secret for seasoned jet-setters.

The remote location in the tropical jungles of Brazil coupled with panoramic ocean views must number among the most stunning of backdrops to your beach and pool. The interior design is as rich in detail as the entire resort.Guest rooms are swathed in natural colours and rustic materials to emphasize the ecological beauty around the resort and it's worth noting also that the hotel is environmentally friendly: solar energy is used for all the water heating and re-forestation of native vegetation and natural materials is deployed as a matter of course.

The outstanding accommodation is plush and elegant; packed with the finest linens and toiletries to make guests feel utterly at home, along with all the complimentary mod-cons like Wi-Fi, DVD\CD players not to mention a personal pool with each villa. It goes without saying that the sunsets over the water are priceless...

The Kenoa Villa should give you a pretty good idea of how it feels to live like royalty. Complete with living room, dining room, king-size bed, a bathroom with an indoor garden, a private garden, a heated infinity-edge pool and a lookout point with direct access to the beach, it's the ultimate hideaway.

You'll notice the staff here too - or rather you won't; the team prides itself on providing service without intrusion but with utter devotion.

The Kaamo restaurant boasts the expertise of world-renowned chef, César Santos whose

original dishes feature regularly in the New York Times, accompanied by an eclectic and comprehensive wine list. There is also a raised lounge overflowing with chic cushions and low seating to make guests feel suitably cosy.

Gentle pampering is a common theme throughout; a fact that the spa takes very seriously as you would expect. The treatments focus on all five senses and for effective treatment book a session with a personal trainer. They can ensure your session relates directly to your health and circumstances. In fact, a stay at Kenoa Resort is akin to receiving a massage of the senses- you owe it to yourself!

AWASI **RESORT**
San Pedro de Atacama / Chile

Imagine a trip where days are spent enjoying guided tours of the Atacama Desert; where you get to see the wildlife up close and personal before retiring at the end of the day on a private patio under a starlit sky. This setting is the norm for guests at Awasi Resort in Chile. Awasi takes great pride in being the only Relais & Chateaux property in the Atacama Desert on top of the fact that it is the only lodge in South America to offer 100% private excursions.

There are only eight rooms so you rarely see other people although you will probably run into llamas or chinchillas roaming around!

Guest rooms use the finest stone and wood décor for a rustic, chic feeling, all underneath charming thatched roofs. For dining, there are all-inclusive offers with exquisite

international food in the private restaurant. Of course, the award-winning chefs will make any dish to match your personal preference (or those of your picky four-year-old).

No wonder the Awasi Resort is referred to as an oasis in the desert.

FAENA **HOTEL**

Buenos Aires | *Argentina*

Imagine a hotel that can erase the mundanities of life in the blink of an eye. Welcome to Faena Hotel - designed as a tribute to the lavish style of the Belle-Epoque age; expect nothing short of magnificent.

Faena Hotel is located in an historic building - in the highly desirable Puerto Madero neighbourhood - that has been completely transformed into a modern masterpiece. The setting combines Argentine influences with magnificent crystal mirrors, imperial furniture and deep red accents to make visitors feel as if they are entering a dream.

There is more to this hotel than pleasing aesthetics though. The beautiful Library Lounge has a bookcase during the day that opens up and turns into a lively bar by night. A grand piano is open to all guests who wish to play, but you may have

some big shoes to fill because Chris Martin from Coldplay composed a song on this piano.

Feeling jet-lagged? The breathtaking spa offers special treatments designed to soothe guests arriving from long trips.

What's more, Faena Hotel is one of the only hotels in the city with an outdoor pool. It is enclosed in terraced gardens, making it the perfect place to work on a tan while snacking on light meals and cocktails.

After lounging by the pool, there is the very best shopping, eating and art that Buenos Aires has to offer just walking distance from the hotel.

So enjoy a holiday full of culture and glamour at its absolute best.

EOLO
Santa Cruz | Argentina

It's hard to believe you're just an hour from Glaciers Natural Park and close to the national airport as you contemplate the peaceful beauty of Eolo. This stunning setting graces the Patagonian steppe with a sense of style and exclusivity surrounded by an enormous expanse of breath-taking natural landscape. With its 17 suites, it offers luxurious accommodation with a remarkably complete service that offers concierge facilities perfect for discovering and dipping into the Patagonian way of life.

Designed in a simple style inspired by the utilitarian architecture of Patagonian "estancias", all the rooms and common areas are furnished with a mixture of modern and antique pieces and boast exceptional views overlooking the steppe, lakes, mountains and glaciers.

Another unique feature is the exceptional staff. They have an unpretentious and flexible approach to service – from the moment you arrive you'll be greeted by name and the team will see to it that you feel utterly at home day and night.

Every activity and detail here is simply delivered to emphasize the purity of the location and its traditions and riches. Arrangements for outdoor activities can be made at the property and there's something for everyone with trekking, bird watching, mountain bike and horse riding courtesy of the expert host guides. We especially recommend a boat trip out to the spectacular glaciers and the four-wheel drive expeditions cross-country. Eolo setting lends itself so well to serious relaxation with a sauna, indoor heated pool and even a well stocked library for enlightened contemplation.

DIRECTORY

EOLO – PATAGONIA'S SPIRIT
190_191 / ARGENTINA

*Ruta Provincial N°11 KM 23, El
Calafate, Santa Cruz, Patagonia
+54 11 4700 0075*

*eolo.com.ar
reservas@eolo.com.ar*

FAENA HOTEL
189 / ARGENTINA

*Martha Salotti 445
Buenos Aires
+54 11 4010 9000*

*faenahotelanduniverse.com
BA-GM@faenahotels.com*

QUALIA
148_149 / AUSTRALIA

*Great Barrier Reef, 20 Whitsunday Boulevard
Hamilton Island Queensland 4803
+1300 780 959*

*qualia.com.au
reservations@qualia.com.au*

HOTEL ARLBERG
36 / AUSTRIA

*6764 Lech am Arlberg, Vorarlberg
+43 5583 2134-0*

*arlberghotel.at/en
info@arlberghotel.at*

AMANKORA
116 / BHUTAN

*Paro, Thimphu, Punakha, Gangtey
Bumthang
+975 8 272 333*

*amanresorts.com
amankora@amanresorts.com*

UMA BY COMO
117 / BHUTAN

*PO Box 222 Paro
+975 8 271 597*

*comohotels.com/umapunakha
uma.punakha@comohotels.com*

DPNY BEACH HOTEL
185 / BRAZIL

*7668, Av Jose Pacheco do Nascimento,
Sao Paulo
+55 12 3894 3000*

*dpny.com
reservas@dpnybeach.com.br*

KENOA RESORT
186_187 / BRAZIL

*Rua Escritor Jorge de Lima, 58, Barramar,
57180-000, Barra de Sao Miguel AL
+55 82 3272 1285*

*kenoaresort.com
info@kenoaresort.com*

POUSADA ESTRELA D´ÁGUA
184 / BRAZIL

*Estrada Arraial D´Ajuda, Trancoso, 45810-000
+55 11 3848 9197*

*estreladagua.com
reservas@estreladagua.com.br*

TXAI RESORT
182_183 / BRAZIL

*Rua Frei Caneca, 1199 Cerquiera
Cesar, Sao Paulo
+55 11 2627 6363*

*txai.com.br
centraldereservas@txairesort.com.br*

CLAYOQUOT WILDERNESS RESORT
159 / CANADA

*P.O. Box 130, 380 Main Street, Tofino,
British Columbia, V0R 2Z0
+1 250 726 8235*

*wildretreat.com
sales@wildretreat.com*

FAIRMONT PACIFIC RIM
156_157 / CANADA

*1038 Canada Place, Vancouver, British
Columbia, Canada, V6C 0B9
+1 604 695 5300*

*fairmont.com/pacific-rim-vancouver
pacificrim@fairmont.com*

SPARKLING HILL RESORT
158 / CANADA

888 Sparkling Place, Vernon,
British Columbia, V1H 2K7
+1 250 275 1556

sparklinghill.com
reservations@sparklinghill.com

AMANYARA
176 / CARIBBEAN

Providenciales, Turks and Caicos
Islands, British West Indies
+1 649 941 8133

amanresorts.com
amanyara@amanresorts.com

CANOUAN RESORT & THE GRENADINES ESTATE VILLAS
180_181 / CARIBBEAN

Canouan Island, St. Vincent and The
Grenadines, British West Indies
+1 784 458 8000

canouanresort.tv
reservations@canouan.com

CAP JULUCA
178_179 / CARIBBEAN

Maundays Bay AI-2640, Anguilla,
British West Indies
+1 264 497 6666

capjuluca.com
capjuluca@capjuluca.com

NECKER ISLAND
174_175 / CARIBBEAN

Virgin Gorda, British Virgin Islands
+44 208 600 0430

neckerisland.com
enquiries@virginlimitededition.com

PARROT CAY BY COMO
177 / CARIBBEAN

PO Box 164, Providenciales, Turks and
Caicos Islands, British West Indies
+1 649 946-7788

comohotels.com/parrotcay
parrotcay@comohotels.com

AWASI
188 / CHILE

Tocopilla 4, San Pedro de Atacama
+44 808 101 6778

awasi.com
info@awasi.cl

CHINA WORLD SUMMIT WING
118_119 / CHINA

No.1 Jianguomenwai Avenue, Beijing 100004
+86 10 6505 2299

shangri-la.com
cwsw@shangri-la.com

FUCHUN RESORT HANGZHOU
121 / CHINA

No 339, Jiangbin Dongdadao, Dongzhou
Jiedao, Fuyang, Hangzhou, Zhejiang 311 401
+86 571 6346 1111

fuchunresort.com
reservation@fuchunresort.com

ISLAND SHANGRI-LA
121 / CHINA

Pacific Place, Supreme Court
Road, Central, Hong Kong
+852 2877 3838

shangri-la.com
isl@shangri-la.com

ST. REGIS BEIJING
120 / CHINA

21 Jianguomenwai Dajie, Beijing, Beijing 100020
+86 10 6460 6688

starwoodhotels.com/stregis
beijing.butler@stregis.com

THE PENINSULA HONG KONG
122_123 / CHINA

Salisbury Road, Kowloon, Hong Kong
+852 2920 2888

hongkong.peninsula.com
phk@peninsula.com

CONSTANTINOU BROS ASIMINA SUITES HOTEL
31 / CYPRUS

Poseidonos Avenue, P.O. Box 60182, Pafos
+357 2696 4333

asimina-cbh.com
reservations@asimina-cbh.com

ALMYRA
30 / CYPRUS

P.O. Box 60136, 8125 Pafos
+357 26 888 700

almyra.com
almyra@thanoshotels.com

ANASSA
29 / CYPRUS

P.O. Box 66006, 8830 Polis
+357 26 888 000

anassa.com
anassa@thanoshotels.com

ROCCO FORTE AUGUSTINE HOTEL
25 / CZECH REPUBLIC

Letenská 12/33, 118 00 Praha 1, Prague
+42 0 266 11 22 33

theaugustine.com
info.augustine@roccofortehotels.com

LE MANOIR AUX QUAT'SAISONS
12_13 / ENGLAND

Church Rd, Great Milton, Oxford, OX44 7PD
+44 1844 278 881

manoir.com

SAN DOMENICO HOUSE
18 / ENGLAND

31 Draycott Place, London, SW3 2SH
+44 2075 815 757

sandomenicohouse.com
info@sandomenicohouse.com

THE CONNAUGHT
15 / ENGLAND

16 Carlos Place, Mayfair, London, W1K 2AL
+44 2074 997 070

the-connaught.co.uk
info@the-connaught.co.uk

THE HALKIN BY COMO
20 / ENGLAND

Halkin Street, Belgravia, London SW1X 7DJ
+44 2073 331 00

comohotels.com/thehalkin
thehalkin@comohotels.com

THE KENSINGTON
19 / ENGLAND

109-113 Queen's Gate, London SW7 5LP
+44 2075 896 300

*doylecollection.com/locations/london_*
city_hotels/the_kensington_hotel.aspx
kensington@doylecollection.com

THE MILESTONE HOTEL
16_17 / ENGLAND

1 Kensington Court, London W8 5DL
+44 20 7917 1000

milestonehotel.com
bookms@rchmail.com

ROCCO FORTE'S BROWN'S HOTEL
14 / ENGLAND

Albemarle Street, Mayfair, London, W1S 4BP
+44 20 7493 6020

brownshotel.com
reservations.browns@roccofortehotels.com

CHÂTEAU DE BAGNOLS
59 / FRANCE

69620 Bagnols
+33 474 71 40 00

chateaudebagnols.com
info@chateaudebagnols.com

GRAND-HOTEL DU CAP-FERRAT
56_57 / FRANCE

71 Bd du General de Gaulle, Saint-Jean Cap-Ferrat, 06230
+33 4.93 76 50 50

grand-hotel-cap-ferrat.com
reservation@ghcf.fr

LE BRISTOL PARIS
56_57 / FRANCE

112 rue de Faubourg Saint Honore, 75008, Paris
+33 1 53 43 43 00

lebristolparis.com
cpelletier@lebristolparis.com

LE BURGUNDY PARIS
64_65 / FRANCE

6-8, rue Duphot, 75001, Paris
+33 1 42 60 34 12

leburgundy.com
sales@leburgundy.com

LE MEURICE, DORCHESTER COLLECTION
68 / FRANCE

228 rue de Rivoli, 75001 Paris, France
+33 1 44 58 10 10

lemeurice.com
reservations.lmp@dorchestercollection.com

LES SUITES DE LA POTINIÈRE HOTEL & SPA
60 / FRANCE

Rue de Plantret, 73120 Courchevel
+33 479 08 00 16

suites-potiniere.com
hotel@suites-potiniere.com

MANDARIN ORIENTAL PARIS
67 / FRANCE

251 rue Saint-Honoré, 75001, Paris
+33 1 70.98 78 88

mandarinoriental.com
mopar-sales@mohg.com

ROYAL-RIVIERA HOTEL
58 / FRANCE

3 Avenue Jean Monnet, Saint-Jean Cap-Ferrat, 06230
+33 4.93 76 31 00

royal-riviera.com
resa@royal-riviera.com

SHANGRI-LA HOTEL PARIS
56_57 / FRANCE

10 avenue d'Iéna, 75116 Paris
+33 1 53 67 19 98

shangri-la.com
slpr@shangri-la.com

TRIANON PALACE VERSAILLE
61 / FRANCE

1 Boulevard de la Reine, 78000 Versailles
+33 1 30 84 50 00

trianonpalace.com

DANAI BEACH RESORT & VILLAS
32_33 / GREECE

1 Nikiti Halkidiki Nikiti 630 88
+30 23750-20400

danairesort.com
info@danairesort.com

GRACE SANTORINI
31 / GREECE

Imerovigli 84700, Thira 847 00
+30 22860-21300

santorinigrace.com
res@santorinigrace.com

Front cover image supplied By Grace Santorini

ANANDA IN THE HIMALAYAS
109 / INDIA

The Palace Estate, Narendra Nagar, Tehri - Garhwal, Uttaranchal - 249175
+91 1378 227 500

anandaspa.com
reservation@anandaspa.com

AMANKILA
117 / INDONESIA

Manggis Candidasa Bali, Indonesia
+62 3634 1333

amanresorts.com/amankila
reservations@amanresorts.com

THE MULIA - NUSA DUA, BALI
144_145 / INDONESIA

Jl. Raya Nusa Dua Selatan, Kawasan Sawangan, Nusa Dua 80363 Bali
+62 361 301 7777

themulia.com
info@themulia.com

ST REGIS BALI
143 / INDONESIA

Kawasan Pariwisata, Nusa Dua Lot S6, PO Box 44, Nusa Dua, Bali 80363
+62 361 8478 111

stregisbali.com

W RETREAT AND SPA BALI – SEMINYAK
146 / INDONESIA

Jl. Petitenget, Seminyak, Bali 80361
+62 361 473 8106

whotels.com/baliseminyak
whotels.bali@whotels.com

CAESAR AUGUSTUS
49 / ITALY

Via G.Orlandi, 4 - 80071 Anacapri, Isle of Capri
+39 081 837 3395

ceasar-augustus.com
info@caesar-augustus.com

CASTELLO DI CASOLE
46 / ITALY

Castello di Casole, Località Querceto, 53031 Casole d'Elsa, Siena
+39.0577.961508

castellodicasole.com
infoeurope@castellodicasole.com

CASTIGLION DEL BOSCO
47 / ITALY

Castiglion del Bosco, 53024, Montalcino, Italy
+39 057 7191 3001

castigliondelbosco.com
info@castigliondelbosco.com

GRAND HOTEL TREMEZZO
44_45 / ITALY

Via Regina, 8 - 22019 Tremezzo, Lago di Como
+39 0344 42491

grandhoteltremezzo.com
info@grandhoteltremezzo.com

HOTEL DANIELI
50_51 / ITALY

Castello 4196, Venice, 30122
+39 041 522 6480

danielihotelvenice.com
danieli@luxurycollection.com

HOTEL D'INGHILTERRA
53 / ITALY

Via Bocca di Leone 14, Rome, 00187
+ 39 06 699 811

hoteldinghilterra.warwickhotels.com
reservation.hir@royaldemeure.com

HOTEL GRITTI PALACE
52 / ITALY

Campo Santa Maria del Giglio, 2467 - 30124 Venezia
+39 041 296 1222

thegrittipalace.com
grittipalace@luxurycollection.com

IL PELLICANO
48 / ITALY

Località Sbarcatello, 58018 Porto Ercole, Grosseto
+39 0564 858 111

pellicano.com
info@pellicanohotel.com

LA POSTA VECCHIA HOTEL
54 / ITALY

Palo Laziale, 00055, Ladispoli, Roma
+39 069 949 501

lapostavecchia.com
reservations@lapostavecchia.com

MASSERIA SAN DOMENICO
55 / ITALY

Strada Litoranea 379, 72015
Savelletri di Fasano, Brindisi
+39 080 482 7769

masseriasandomenico.com
info@masseriasandomenico.com

PALACE HOTEL TOKYO
112_115 / JAPAN

1-1-1 Marunouchi, Chiyoda-ku, Tokyo, 100-0005
+81 332115211

palacehoteltokyo.com

EXPLOREANS MARA RIANTA CAMP
91 / KENYA

Cismara Koiyaki Dagurugurueiti,
P.O. Box 741, Narok
+ 254 788 262 666

marariantacamp.exploreans.com
info.mara@exploreans.com

TRIBE HOTEL
92_93 / KENYA

Limuru Road, The Village Market,
Gigiri, Nairobi, 00621
+254 20 720 0000

tribe-hotel.com
stay@tribehotel-kenya.com

MZIMA
94 / KENYA

Gala Beach, Ukunda 80400
+254 0 703 773499

mzima.co.ke
info@mzima.co.ke

BANYAN TREE MADIVARU
105 / MALDIVES

AA. Ethere Madivaru, North Ari Atoll
+960 666 0760

banyantree.com/en/maldives_madivaru
reservations-madivaru@banyantree.com

BAROS MALDIVES
103 / MALDIVES

P.O. Box 2015, Male' 20-02
+960 664 26 72

baros.com
info@baros.com

COCO BODU HITHI
104 / MALDIVES

Bodu Hithi Island, North Malé Atoll
+ 960 664 1122

cocoboduhithi.com
reservations@cococollection.com.mv

JUMEIRAH DHEVANAFUSHI
106 / MALDIVES

Meradhoo Island, Gaafu Alifu Atoll
+960 682 8800

jumeirah.com
jumeirahdhevanafushi@jumeirah.com

JUMEIRAH VITTAVELI
102 / MALDIVES

Bolifushi Island, South Male Atoll
+960 682 8800

jumeirah.com
jumeirahvittaveli@jumeirah.com

PARK HYATT MALDIVES HADAHAA
100_101 / MALDIVES

North Huvadhoo, Gaafu Alifu Atoll
+960 682 1234

maldives.hadahaa.park.hyatt.com
maldives.parkhadahaa@hyatt.com

**SHANGRI-LA'S VILLINGILI
RESORT AND SPA MALDIVES**
98_99 / MALDIVES

Villingili Island, Addu Atoll
+ 960 689 7888

shangri-la.com
slmd@shangri-la.com

MARADIVA VILLAS RESORT AND SPA
96 / MAURITIUS

Wolmar, Flic en Flac
+230 403 1500

maradiva.com
reservations@maradiva.com

ST. REGIS MAURITIUS
97 / MAURITIUS

Le Morne Peninsula
+230 403 9000

stregismauritius.com
sales.mauritius@stregis.com

CUIXMALA
173 / MEXICO

KM 46.2 Carretera Melaque-Puerto
Vallarta, Jalisco, 48893
+ 52 312316 0300

cuixmala.com
reservations@cuixmala.com

ESENCIA ESTATE
172 / MEXICO

Carretera Cancún-Tulum, Predio Rústico
Xpu-Ha lotes 18 y 19, Xpu-Ha 77710
+52 984 873 4830

hotelesencia.com
reservations@hotelesencia.com

AMAN SVETI STEFAN
35 / MONTENEGRO

Sveti Stefan 85315, Montenegro
+382 33 420 000

amanresorts.com
reservations@amanresorts.com

BLANKET BAY
150_151 / NEW ZEALAND

Rapid 4191 Glenorchy
+64 3 441 0115

blanketbay.com
information@blanketbay.com

EAGLES NEST
152_153 / NEW ZEALAND

60 Tapeka Road, Russell 0242, Bay of Islands
+64 9 403 8333

www.eaglesnest.co.nz
res@eaglesnest.co.nz

SHANGRI-LA'S BORACAY RESORT & SPA
137 / PHILIPPINES

Barangay Yapak, Boracay
Island, Malay Aklan 5608
+63 36 288 4988

shangri-la.com/boracay/boracayresort

PINE CLIFFS TERRACES & VILLAS
69 / PORTUGAL

Praia da Falésia, Apt. 644, 8200-
909 Albufeira, Algarve
+351 289 500 100

pinecliffsportugal.com
reservations@pinecliffsportugal.com

ARARAT PARK HYATT MOSCOW
24 / RUSSIA

4 Neglinnaya Street, Moscow, 109012
+7 495 783 1234

moscow.park.hyatt.com
moscow.park@hyatt.com

PARK HYATT JEDDAH
82 / SAUDI ARABIA

Al Kurnaysh Rd, Al Hamra, Jeddah
+02 263 9666

jeddah.park.hyatt.com
jeddah.park@hyatt.com

FRÉGATE ISLAND PRIVATE
95 / SEYCHELLES

P.O. Box 330 Victoria, Mahé
+248 4 670 100

fregate.com
reservations@fregate.com

SHANGRI-LA SINGAPORE
139 / SINGAPORE

22 Orange Grove Road, Singapore, 258350
+65 6737 3644

shangri-la.com/singapore/shangrila

THE FULLERTON BAY HOTEL
142 / SINGAPORE

80 Collyer Quay, Singapore, 049326
+65 6333 8388

fullertonbayhotel.com
info@fullertonbayhotel.com

THE FULLERTON HOTEL
138 / SINGAPORE

1 Fullerton Square, Singapore, 049178
+65 6733 8388

fullertonhotel.com
info@fullertonhotel.com

W SINGAPORE SENTOSA COVE
140 / SINGAPORE

21 Ocean Way, Singapore, 098374
+65 6808 7288

wsingaporesentosacove.com
whotels.singapore@whotels.com

PEZULA PRIVATE CASTLE
84_85 / SOUTH AFRICA

Lagoonview Drive, Eastern Head,
Knysna, Western Cape
+27 44 302 3333

conradpezula.com
conradpezula.reservations@conradhotels.com

KENSINGTON PLACE
83 / SOUTH AFRICA

Higgovale, Cape Town, 8001
+27 21 424 4744

kensingtonplace.co.za
reception@kensingtonplace.co.za

SINGITA BOULDERS LODGE
86 / SOUTH AFRICA

Sabi Sand Private Game Reserve
+27 21 683 3424

singita.com
reservations@singita.com

FINCA CORTESIN HOTEL & GOLF
74_75 / SPAIN

Carretera de Casares, Km 2,
29690 Casares, Málaga
+34 952 93 78 00

fincacortesin.com
reservas@hotelcortesin.com

HOTEL HACIENDA NA XAMENA
72_73 / SPAIN

Buzón 11, Na Xamena, 07815 San Miguel, Ibiza
+34 971 33 45 00

hotelhacienda-ibiza.com
info@hotelhacienda-ibiza.com

SHA WELLNESS CLINIC
70_71 / SPAIN

Verderol 5 El Albir, 0358, 1 Alicante
+34 966 81 11 99

shawellnessclinic.com
info@shawellnessclinic.com

ADITYA
107 / SRI LANKA

719/1, Galle Road, Devenigoda,
Rathgama, Galle
+94 91 2267 708

aditya-resort.com
adityavilla@sltnet.lk

THE FORTRESS RESORT & SPA
108 / SRI LANKA

PO Box 126, Galle
+94 91 438 940

thefortress.lk
info@thefortress.lk

ICEHOTEL
22 / SWEDEN

Marknadsvägen 63, 981 91 Jukkasjärvi
+46 980 668 00

icehotel.com
info@icehotel.com

Photo Credits

Art Deco Suite, Photo: Leif Milling, Artists:
Tomasz Czajkowski & Eryk Marks.

Bubblesuite, Photo: Leif Milling, Artists:
Wilfred Stijger & Edith van de Wetering.

Royal Deluxe Suite, Photo: Christopher Hauser.
Artists: Marinus Vroom & Marjolein Vonk.

LYDMAR HOTEL
21 / SWEDEN

Södra Blasieholmshamnen 2, 103 24 Stockholm
46 08 22 31 60

lydmar.com
reservations@lydmar.com

TREEHOTEL
23 / SWEDEN

Edeforsväg 2 A, 960 24 Harads
+46 928 104 03

treehotel.se
info@treehotel.se

CARLTON HOTEL ST MORITZ
37 / SWITZERLAND

St. Moritz, Switzerland
+41 81 836 70 00

carlton-stmoritz.ch
info@carlton-stmoritz.ch

GRAND HOTEL BELLEVUE
40 / SWITZERLAND

Untergstaadstrasse 11 3780
+41 33 748 00 00

bellevue-gstaad.com
info@bellevue-gstaad.ch

GSTAAD PALACE
39 / SWITZERLAND

CH-3780 Gstaad
+41 33 748 50 00

palace.ch
info@palace.ch

HOTEL D'ANGLETERRE
42_43 / SWITZERLAND

Quai du Mont-Blanc 17, 1201 Geneva
+41 22 906 5555

dangleterrehotel.com
bookan@rchmail.com

LES TROIS ROIS
41 / SWITZERLAND

Blumenrain 8, 4001 Basel
+41 61 260 50 50

lestroisrois.com
info@lestroisrois.com

PARK HYATT ZURICH
38 / SWITZERLAND

Beethoven-Strasse 21, 8002 Zurich
+41 043 883 12 34

zurich.park.hyatt.com
zurich.park@hyatt.com

DIAMONDS STAR OF EAST
90 / TANZANIA

P.O. Box 2019, Nungwi Road, Zanzibar
+ 255 24 2240175

staroftheeast.diamonds-resorts.com
info.sote@diamonds-resorts.com

SINGITA FARU FARU LODGE
88_89 / TANZANIA

Grumeti Reserves
+27 21 683 3424

singita.com
reservations@singita.com

AMANPURI
130 / THAILAND

Pansea Beach, Phuket 83000
+94 112 035 700

amanresorts.com
reservations@amanresorts.com

INDIGO PEARL
129 / THAILAND

Nai Yang Beach and National Park,
Phuket 83110
+66 76 327 006

indigo-pearl.com
info@indigo-pearl.com

PARESA RESORT
125 / THAILAND

49 Moo 6, Layi-Nakalay Road,
Kamala , Phuket, 83150
+66 76 302 000

paresaresorts.com
info@paresaresorts.com

SILAVADEE POOL SPA & RESORT
132_133 / THAILAND

208/66 Moo 4, Maret, Koh
Samui, Suratthani 84310
+66 77 960 555

www.silavadeeresort.com
info@silavadeeresort.com

ST. REGIS BANGKOK
131 / THAILAND

159 Rajadamri Road, Bangkok 10330
+66 02-207 7777

www.starwoodhotels.com/stregis
butler.bangkok@stregis.com

THE NAKA ISLAND – A LUXURY COLLECTION RESORT & SPA
128 / THAILAND

32 Moo 5, Tambon Paklok, Amphur
Thalang Naka Yai Island, Phuket 83110
+66 76 371 400

www.nakaislandphuket.com

THE RACHA
126_127 / THAILAND

42/12-13 Moo 5, Rawai, Muang, Phuket, 83130
+66 76 355 455

theracha.com
reservation@racha.com

MUSEUM HOTEL
26_27 / TURKEY

Tekeli mah. No:1 Uchisar, Nevsehir
+90 384 219 2220

museum-hotel.com
info@museumhotel.com.tr

THE SOFA HOTEL
28 / TURKEY

Tesvikiye Caddesi No 41-41A,
34367 Nisantasi, Istanbul
+90 212 368 1818

thesofahotel.com
info@thesofahotel.com

AL MAHA DESERT RESORT
80 / UNITED ARAB EMIRATES

Dubai Desert Conservation Reserve - Dubai
+971 4 832 9900

al-maha.com
reservation.almaha@luxurycollection.com

ARMANI HOTEL DUBAI
78_79 / UNITED ARAB EMIRATES

P.O. Box 888333, Dubai
+971 4 888 3888

www.dubai.armanihotels.com
info@armanihotels.com

ST. REGIS SAADIYAT
81 / UNITED ARAB EMIRATES

P.O. Box 54345, Abu Dhabi
+971 2 498 8888

stregissaadiyatisland.com
reservations.saadiyat@stregis.com

BLANTYRE
168_169 / USA

16 Blantyre Road, Lenox, MA 01240
+1 413 637 3556

blantyre.com
welcome@blantyre.com

COLONY PALMS HOTEL
170_171 / USA

572 N. Indian Canyon Drive,
Palm Springs, CA 92262
+1 760 969 1800

colonypalmshotel.com
info@colonypalmshotel.com

MANDARIN ORIENTAL NEW YORK
162 / USA

80 Columbus Circle New York, NY 10023
+1 212 805 8800

mandarinoriental.com/newyork
monyc-reservations@mohg.com

ST. REGIS NEW YORK
163 / USA

2 East 55th Street New York, NY 10022
+1 212 753 4500

stregisnewyork.com

THE BETSY HOTEL
166 / USA

1440 Ocean Drive, Miami Beach, FL 33139
+1 305 531 6100

thebetsyhotel.com
info@thebetsyhotel.com

THE CHATWAL – A LUXURY COLLECTION
160 / USA

130 West 44th street, New York, NY 10036
+1 212 764 6200

thechatwalny.com

THE PLAZA
161 / USA

768 5th Avenue New York, NY 10019
+1 212 759 3000

theplaza.com

THE SETAI MIAMI BEACH
164_165 / USA

2001 Collins Avenue, Miami, FL 33139
+1 305 520 6000

thesetaihotel.com
reservations@thesetaihotel.com

W SOUTH BEACH
167 / USA

2201 Collins Ave, Miami Beach, FL 33139
+1 305 938 3000

wsouthbeach.com

FUSION MAIA DA NANG
134_135 / VIETNAM

Truong Sa, Ngũ Hành Son Da Nang, Vietnam
+84 0511 396 7999

fusionmaiadanang.com
reservation-dn@fusion-resorts.com

PRINCESS D'ANNAM RESORT & SPA
136 / VIETNAM

Hon Lan, Tan Thanh Commune, Ham Thuan
Nam District, Binh Thuan Province, Vietnam
+84 62 3682 222

princessannam.com
info@princessannam.com

1.

2.

Q QUINTESSENTIALLY
PUBLISHING

www.quintessentiallypublishing.com

info@quintessentiallypublishing.com   +44 (0)20 3073 6845

4.

3.

.Publishing

www.quintessentiallycreative.com

info@quintessentiallycreative.com   +44(0) 20 3073 6719

QUINTESSENTIALLY
CREATIVE

LUXURY BRAND
CONSULTANCY
BRANDING
DESIGN
PACKAGING TV
PUBLISHING
DIGITAL
MARKETING
PHOTOGRAPHY
GLOBAL
MARKETING
TOOLS PR
EVENT
MANAGEMENT
PRODUCTION

WE CONNECT BRANDS TO PEOPLE, PEOPLE TO BRANDS

*The ultimate resource for the discerning
private jet traveller*

ESCAPE

*Experiences that push the boundaries
of your imagination*

TRAVEL

*Creating tailor-made holidays
the world over*

VILLAS

*An elite collection of luxury
residences across the globe*

ACKNOWLEDGEMENTS

Thank you to all our hotel partners who so gracefully allowed us access to their images and stories in this book. Quintessentially Design led by *Chris Charalambous*, *Giorgio Criscione* and *William Parry*, put in hours of painstaking work to ensure the book looks as beautiful as ever. Thank you to *Hallie Bird* who managed the project and the relationships with hotels, *Christopher Rayner*, who oversaw the beginning of the process before moving on to pastures new, the in-house editorial team headed up by *Nathalie Bradbury* with the help of Top Editor *Peter Archer* along with *Alice Goss*, *Georgie Lane-Godfrey*, *Rachel Bailin*, *Hilary Burns*, *Angela Stobaugh* and *Michael Hurley*. Michael assisted *Lois Crompton*, our Head of Production on the logistics of creating the book, *Will Sutton* looked after distribution and *Tom Parker* advised on sales.

Final thanks to *Rebecca Tucker* and *Aaron Simpson* for constant support.

We look forward to seeing Quintessentially Reserve 2013 in book stores and in your homes.

Quintessentially Publishing Ltd.
29 Portland Place, London, W1B 1QB
Tel +44 (0)20 3073 6845
production@quintessentiallypublishing.com
www.quintessentiallypublishing.com

ISBN: 978-0-9569952-6-1